Editorial Project Manager
Lorin E. Klistoff, M.A.

Illustrator
Blanca Apodaca

Cover Artist
Brenda DiAntonis

Managing Editor
Karen J. Goldfluss, M.S. Ed.

Creative Director
Karen J. Goldfluss, M.S. Ed.

Art Production Manager
Kevin Barnes

Art Coordinator
Renée Christine Yates

Imaging
James Edward Grace

Publisher
Mary D. Smith, M.S. Ed.

Christian

Grades 1-4

Bulletin Board
Ideas and Patterns

Holidays and Seasons

THE AUTUMN SEASON IS FULL OF REASONS TO HONOR GOD

Honor the Lord with...the firstfruits of all your crops.
Proverbs 3:9

Author

Mary Tucker

Teacher Created Resources, Inc.
12621 Western Avenue
Garden Grove, CA 92841
www.teachercreated.com
ISBN: 978-1-4206-7070-7
©2006 Teacher Created Resources, Inc.
Reprinted, 2016
Made in U.S.A.

Teacher Created Resources

CHRISTIAN DIVISION

Table of Contents

Table of Contents

Introduction

Well planned and executed bulletin boards can have a powerful impact on children in elementary grades. Even simple ones can grab children's attention and teach important truths with a minimum of words. Of course, children learn best by doing, so most of the bulletin boards in this book include student participation. Each idea includes not only a list of materials needed and step-by-step directions for assembling the board, but also suggested activity ideas: discussion questions, simple crafts, songs, games, action rhymes, looking up and reading verses in the Bible (*Note:* This book uses the New International Version.), and a variety of other correlated activities.

The bulletin boards include creative ideas for: looking back at what God did in the past year and looking forward to God's work in the New Year, discovering where love comes from on Valentine's Day, personalizing Jesus' death for our sins on Good Friday, remembering that the real message of Easter is that God loves us, thinking about ways to show love for Mom on Mother's Day and throughout the year, considering what makes a good dad on Father's Day, and understanding how faith in God can make the new school year cool!

Encourage children to ask questions if they do not understand something on a bulletin board. If it is a Bible question, do not just tell them the answer. Help them look up the answer in the Bible and read it for themselves. Be sure to read each bulletin board together; then ask your children to share their ideas about what it teaches and how it relates to the holiday or season it celebrates. Use each bulletin board as a springboard for discussion and to focus student attention on God's truths.

Patterns are provided for each bulletin board. Some may be used for more than one bulletin board. Enlarge them as necessary for greater impact, depending on the size of your bulletin board. This can easily be done on a copier, though you may have to copy a pattern in sections, then put it together on the board. If you feel you are artistically challenged, use the letter patterns at the back of the book to create the word messages on the bulletin boards.

Do not leave the holiday bulletin boards up too long after the holiday is over. If possible, take each one down promptly and put up other general topic boards until the next holiday comes around. If you need ideas for other kinds of bulletin boards, check out TCR 7027 *Christian Bulletin Board Idea Book*.

Every Day Is a New Beginning that God Has Planned for You!

"For I know the plans I have for you," declares the Lord, "plans to prosper you and not to harm you, plans to give you hope and a future." (Jeremiah 29:11)

Materials

- green background paper
- white paper
- yellow paper *(optional)*
- markers (black and colors)
- patterns on pages 6 and 7
- tape or stapler
- scissors

Directions

1. Cover the board with green paper.
2. Print the caption at the top of the board and the Bible verse at the bottom.
3. Enlarge the patterns. Color the hen and chick yellow or copy them on yellow paper.
4. Attach the hen to the center of the board with the chick close by.
5. Attach the hatchling to the left side of the board.
6. Cut out an egg for each child and hand them out.
7. Have the children write their birthdays on their eggs, then attach them to the bulletin board.

Suggested Activities

- Discuss the Bible verse. Ask children what they think it means. Are God's plans for us in the new year good or bad? God does not say we won't have trouble in the new year, but He promises we will "prosper" or do well.

- Tell or review the Bible story of Joseph. Point out how God watched over him in trouble and blessed him. God's plans for him included both good times and hard times, but God definitely "prospered" him. You will find the story in Genesis 37–45.

- Ask children what they would like to do for the Lord in the coming year. Then take a couple of minutes for them to pray for one another and for God's blessings in the new year.

Patterns

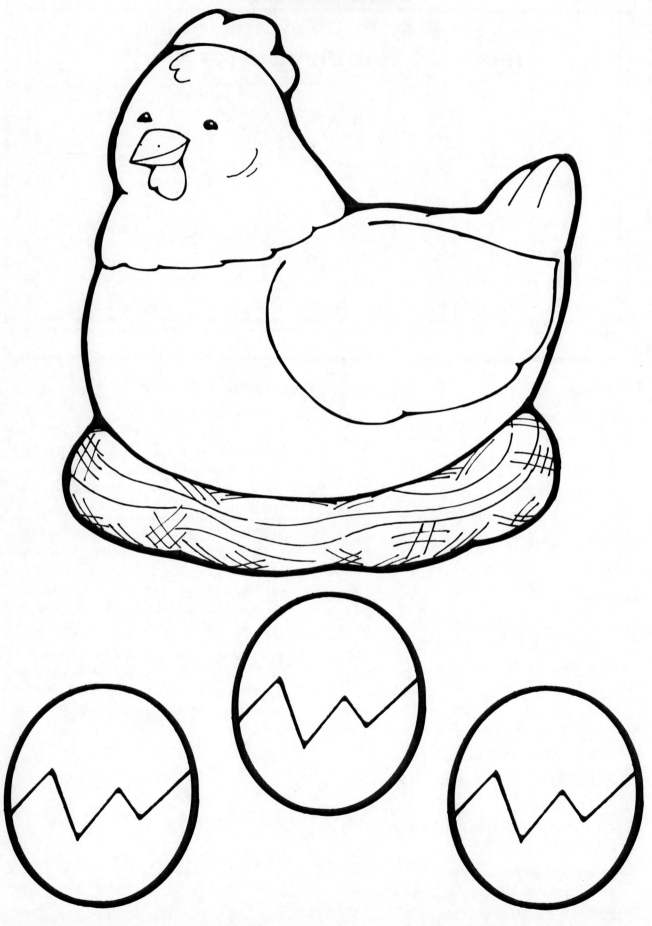

Patterns

Materials

- blue background paper
- colored paper (variety of colors)
- markers (black and colors)
- patterns on pages 9 and 10
- letter patterns on pages 143 and 144 *(optional)*
- tape or stapler
- scissors

Directions

1. Cover the board with blue paper.

2. Print the rhyme at the top of the board in large letters or use the letter patterns on pages 143 and 144.

3. Copy the patterns on pages 9 and 10 on colored paper. Make enough copies of the small fish for each child to have one with some extras.

4. Print the date of the past year with black marker on the big fish and attach it to the board.

5. Attach the starfish and Bible verse clam shell on the board.

6. Give each child a fish and a marker. Have them write things God did for them last year on the fish; then add them to the bulletin board display.

Suggested Activities

- Ask students to tell about the things God did for them that they wrote on their fish. Encourage them to share more details. Pray together, letting them thank God for what He did.

- Children can memorize the Bible verse on the board by singing the words to the tune of "B-I-N-G-O."

    I can say Psalm 77, verse 11a:
    I will remember, I will remember,
    I will remember the deeds of the Lord.

- Serve fish-shaped crackers for a snack. As children eat them, they can say a book of the Bible or word of a Bible verse for each cracker.

Pattern

Patterns

I will remember
the deeds
of the Lord.
(Psalm 77:11a)

Materials

- pink background paper
- red, white, and green paper
- patterns on pages 12 and 13
- letter patterns on pages 143 and 144 *(optional)*
- colored markers
- scissors
- fine-tip markers or pens

Directions

1. Cover the board with pink paper.

2. Print the question on a strip of white paper or use the letter patterns. Add a heart on each end and put it at the top of the board.

3. Enlarge the figure of Jesus on white paper, color it, cut it out, and attach it to the center of the board.

4. Enlarge the door pattern, color it, and cut it in half.

5. Place the closed door over the figure of Jesus. Tape it only on the left and right side so it can be easily opened.

6. Give students heart patterns and red and white paper. Have them cut out heart-shaped flowers.

7. Have each student write a Bible verse about God's love on a heart flower, such as one of the following: Numbers 14:18; 1 Chronicles 16:34; Psalm 32:10; Psalm 86:5; Psalm 145:8; Jeremiah 31:3; Zephaniah 3:17; John 3:16; Romans 5:8; 1 John 4:10.

8. Cut stems and leaves from green paper. Attach the heart flowers next to the door.

9. Open the door to find out where love comes from.

Suggested Activities

- Let students read their verses aloud before putting them on the board.

- Tell Jesus' story of The Lost Son, Luke 15:11–24. Explain that the father represents God and the story is an illustration of how much God loves us.

- Let children make valentines for friends or family, including messages about God's love for them.

Patterns

Dear Friends, let us love one another for love comes from God. Everyone who loves has been born of God and knows God.
(1 John 4:7)

Pattern

A Big Batch of Love to Share with Everyone

Recipe for Love

Ingredients
• Lots of Patience
• Plenty of Kindness

Directions
Mix together with Trust and Hope. Sprinkle with Unselfishness. Serve with Truth.

Remember
Do not include envy, bragging or pride! Rudeness or anger will ruin this recipe.

(Based on 1 Corinthians 13:4–7)

Do everything in love.
(1 Corinthians 16:14)

Materials

- white background paper
- pink, tan, red, and white paper
- patterns on pages 15 and 16
- letter patterns on pages 143 and 144 *(optional)*
- colored markers or crayons
- tape or stapler
- scissors

Directions

1. Cover the board with white paper.

2. Print the caption or use the letter patterns. Attach the caption at the top of the board.

3. Enlarge the pattern of the chef, color it, and cut it out. Attach it to the right side of the board.

4. Copy the Bible verse pattern on tan paper and the large recipe on pink paper, and cut them out. Attach the recipe to the left side of the board and the Bible verse near the chef.

5. Let children cut small hearts from red paper and add them to the bulletin board display as shown.

Suggested Activities

- Read the recipe together and discuss it. Ask a student to read aloud the Bible passage on which it is based. Talk about what love looks like in everyday life.

- Give each student a small copy of the recipe, a paper or Styrofoam™ cup, some glue, and crayons or markers. Have them glue the recipe on the cup, then decorate the cup. Then hand out small colorful candies, such as jellybeans, which they can put in the cups to give a friend or family member.

- Print the letters of the words of the Bible verse, 1 Corinthians 16:14, on red hearts. Lay the hearts in scrambled order on a table. Let children take turns seeing how quickly they can arrange the letter hearts in correct order to spell out the verse. Time them to see who is the fastest.

- Show children how to hold up the thumb, index finger, and little finger to "sign" the word "love." Let them practice saying the Bible verse, 1 Corinthians 16:14, using the sign.

Patterns

Recipe for Love

Ingredients
- Lots of Patience
- Plenty of Kindness

Directions
Mix together with Trust and Hope. Sprinkle with Unselfishness. Serve with Truth.

Remember
Do not include envy, bragging, or pride! Rudeness or anger will ruin this recipe.

(Based on 1 Corinthians 13:4–7)

Do everything in love. (1 Corinthians 16:14)

Recipe for Love

<u>**Ingredients**</u>

- **Lots of Patience**
- **Plenty of Kindness**

<u>**Directions**</u>

Mix together with Trust and Hope. Sprinkle with Unselfishness. Serve with Truth.

<u>**Remember**</u>

Do not include envy, bragging, or pride! Rudeness or anger will ruin this recipe.

(Based on 1 Corinthians 13:4–7)

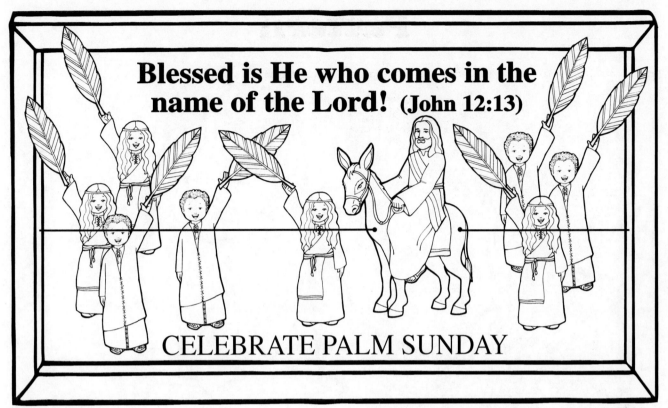

Blessed is He who comes in the name of the Lord! *(John 12:13)*

CELEBRATE PALM SUNDAY

Materials

- yellow background paper
- white and green paper
- patterns on pages 18 and 19
- letter patterns on pages 143 and 144 *(optional)*
- colored markers or crayons
- white cardstock
- scissors
- string
- hole punch
- tape or stapler
- push pins or tacks

Directions

1. Cover the board with yellow paper.

2. Print the caption or use the letter patterns. Attach the caption at the top of the board.

3. Give each child a copy of the boy or girl pattern to color and cut out. Give each one a palm branch copied on green paper to cut out and put in the raised hand of the boy or girl. They can arrange the figures across the board near the top like a crowd lining the street.

4. Copy the figure of Jesus on the donkey on cardstock. Then color and cut it out. Punch two holes in the pattern where indicated.

5. Attach a length of string to one side of the bulletin board and stretch it across to the other side. Insert the string in the holes on the donkey pattern, then fasten it to the edge of the board.

6. Students can take turns moving the figure of Jesus on the donkey across the board as the crowd cheers.

Suggested Activities

- Explain why we celebrate Palm Sunday by telling the story of Jesus' triumphal entry into Jerusalem from Luke 19:28–40. Let children act it out.

- Ask students to describe what they think would happen if Jesus came riding into their town today. What would they do to welcome Him? Would most people be happy to see Him? Why or why not?

Pattern

Patterns

Let Everyone and Everything, Praise the Lord!

If my people did not praise me, the stones would cry out! (see Luke 19:40)

All you have made will praise you, O Lord! (Psalm 145:10a)

Materials

- light blue and green background paper
- white paper
- patterns on pages 21 and 22
- letter patterns on pages 143 and 144 (optional)
- colored markers or crayons
- scissors
- tape or stapler
- leaves

Directions

1. Cover the board with light blue paper. Cover the bottom of the board with green paper.

2. Print the caption and Bible verse or use the letter patterns. Attach them to the board as shown.

3. Enlarge the pattern of Jesus, color it, and cut it out. Attach it to the center of the board.

4. Print Jesus' words above the figure in a speech balloon as shown.

5. Give each child a copy of one or two of the patterns on pages 21 and 22 to color and cut out. Have them attach the items to the board.

6. Attach leaves and some of the small patterns to the outside border.

Suggested Activities

- Read the story of Jesus' entry into Jerusalem from Luke 19:28–40. Emphasize Jesus' reply (verse 40) to some Pharisees who scolded Him for letting His disciples praise Him.

- Point out that all the items on the board praise the Lord, perhaps not with voices or words, but just by existing because He created them. Read Psalm 148 aloud and point to the items as they are mentioned. Challenge students to brainstorm other created things that praise Him just by being what He made them.

- Print the word "PRAISE" vertically on the board. Have students suggest ways we can praise the Lord, using words that begin with the letters on the board. (Example: P-pray, R-read the Bible, A-act the way He wants us to, I-Imitate Jesus, S-sing about Him, E-encourage others to accept Jesus.)

Patterns

Patterns

Who is Good Friday good for?

LIFT AND LOOK
God showed His love for us in this: while we were still sinners, Jesus died for us.
(see Romans

Materials

- dark blue background paper
- tan and green paper
- patterns on pages 24 and 25
- letter patterns on pages 143 and 144 *(optional)*
- scissors
- mirror
- sticky hangers (strong enough to hold the mirror to the board)

Directions

1. Cover the board with dark blue paper.

2. Print the caption question or use the letter patterns. Attach the caption question to the top of the board.

3. Copy the cross and the Bible verse flap on tan paper and cut them out.

4. Cut a hill from green paper.

5. Put the cross on the hill and attach them to the left side of the board.

6. Attach the mirror to the right side of the board. Cover the mirror with the tan Bible verse piece.

7. Let children read the words on the board, then lift the flap to see themselves in the mirror, showing that Good Friday is good for them.

Suggested Activities

- Discuss why Jesus' death on Good Friday is good for us *(because His death paid for our sins)*. We can have forgiveness when we receive Him as Savior. That is why we call it Good Friday.

- Let children make nail crosses. Give each student two large nails and a length of wire. Show them how to hold the nails in the shape of a cross and fasten them together by winding the wire around and around the middle. Younger children may need you to do this for them, or at least get them started. The wire needs to be tightly wound. Loop a thin piece of string and attach it to the top of the nail cross for a hanger.

- Pray together, encouraging students to thank the Lord for dying on the cross for their sins.

Patterns

LIFT AND LOOK

God showed His love for us in this: while we were still sinners, Jesus died for us.

(see Romans 5:8)

Easter Means New Life in Christ!

Jesus is Alive!

Just as Christ was raised from the dead through the glory of the Father, we too may live a new life. (Romans 6:4b)

Materials

- shiny gold or silver background paper
- letter patterns on pages 143 and 144 (*optional*)
- white paper
- strip of cardstock
- patterns on pages 27 and 28
- colored markers or crayons
- colored tissue paper or foil (various colors)
- scissors
- tape or stapler
- glue

Directions

1. Cover the board with gold or silver paper.

2. Cut the letters for the caption from white paper using the letter patterns on pages 143 and 144 or print them on a paper strip and attach them to the board.

3. Enlarge the child pattern. Color it, cut it out, and attach it to the board. Cut out one of the butterflies and color it. Accordion fold a short strip of cardstock. Glue one end to the butterfly and the other end to the child's finger so the butterfly moves.

4. Copy the butterfly patterns and give one to each child to color and cut out.

5. Help younger students cut out the wing sections and glue colored tissue paper or foil to the back to make beautiful wings.

6. Have students write their names on their butterflies, then put them all over the board.

Suggested Activities

- Butterflies are a symbol of new life. Ask students to explain how a caterpillar becomes a butterfly. Explain that Jesus died, then came back to life so those who trust in Him can be born again.

- Sing these words to the tune of "Old MacDonald Had a Farm."

Jesus came to give new life—Hallelujah!
To all those who believe in Him—Hallelujah!
If we believe, we will receive
Life in Him that never ends.
Jesus came to give new life—Hallelujah!

Patterns

Jesus is Alive!

Patterns

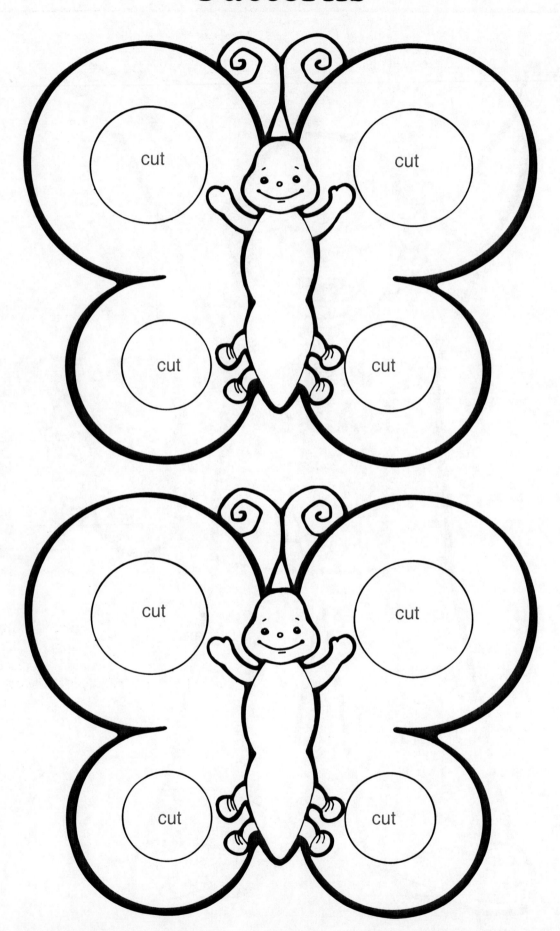

Jesus died and rose again! (1 Thessalonians 4:14a)

Materials

- bright green background paper
- letter patterns on pages 143 and 144 *(optional)*
- white paper and white cardstock
- patterns on page 30 and page 21
- colored markers or crayons
- scissors
- tape or stapler
- construction paper (various colors)

Directions

1. Cover the board with bright green paper.

2. Print the caption and the Bible verse on white strips of paper and attach them to the board. Or, you can trace the letter patterns on pages 143 and 144.

3. Enlarge the two bird patterns. Color them and cut them out. Attach them to the ends of the caption strip as if they are holding it in their beaks.

4. Enlarge the tomb on cardstock. Color it and cut it out. Cut around the door, leaving the left side attached so it can be opened and closed.

5. Enlarge or reduce the pattern of Jesus, page 21, to fit in the tomb. Color and cut it out. Mount it at the center of the board.

6. Attach the tomb over the figure of Jesus.

7. Make additional copies of birds and place them on the board.

8. Hand out construction paper, scissors, and markers or crayons. Let children create flowers and add them around the tomb.

9. Open the tomb to see that Jesus is alive!

Suggested Activities

- Tell the story of Jesus' resurrection from Matthew 28:1–10. Let younger students pantomime how they would have reacted if they had been the women at the tomb. Point out that the tomb on the bulletin board has Jesus in it, alive, but in the Bible story the tomb was empty.

- Ask students how Jesus' resurrection makes a difference in their lives. What if he had stayed dead?

Patterns

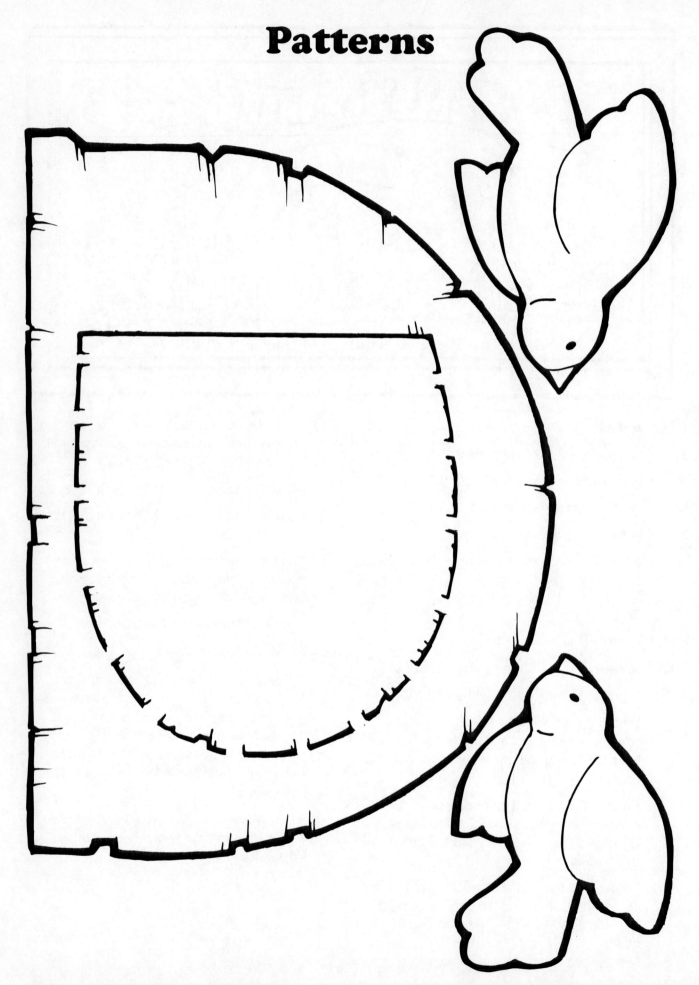

The Message of Easter

This is how God showed his love among us: He sent his one and only Son into the world that we might live through him. (1 John 4:9)

Materials

- lavender background paper
- letter patterns on pages 143 and 144 *(optional)*
- gray and white paper
- patterns on page 32
- colored markers or crayons
- tape or stapler
- scissors

Directions

1. Cover the board with lavender paper.

2. Print the caption or cut out the letters, using the letter patterns. Attach the caption to the top of the board.

3. Print the Bible verse at the bottom of the board.

4. Enlarge the elephant, copying it on gray paper. Copy the sign on white paper. Cut them out.

5. Mount the elephant on the board.

6. Attach the sign to the board, placing it in the curled part of the elephant's trunk.

Suggested Activities

- Explain that elephants are known for their long memories. God wants us to remember that He will always love us. Each year, the story of Jesus' death and resurrection remind us of His love. Let students tell the Easter story.

- Sing these words to the tune of "Mary Had a Little Lamb."

  Just remember God loves you,
  God loves you, God loves you.
  Just remember God loves you,
  And He always will.

  I'll remember God loves me,
  God loves me, God loves me.
  I'll remember God loves me,
  And I love Him too.

- Make reduced copies (about half size) of the elephant pattern. Give each child two. Staple them together at the top to make an Easter card. Have each child write the message "Never forget that God loves you!" on the inside of the card to give to a family member or friend.

Patterns

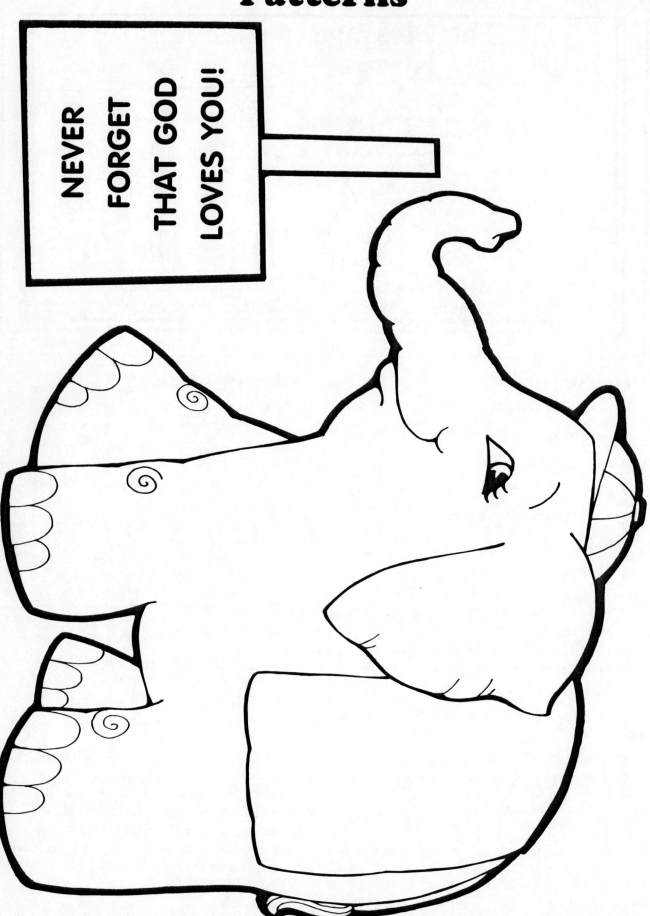

NEVER FORGET THAT GOD LOVES YOU!

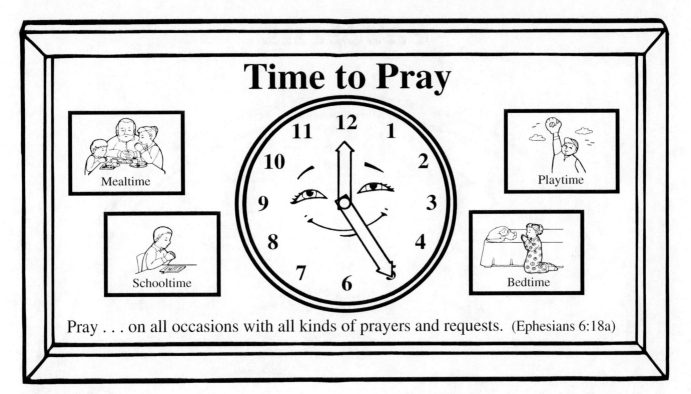

Time to Pray

Mealtime

Playtime

Schooltime

Bedtime

Pray . . . on all occasions with all kinds of prayers and requests. (Ephesians 6:18a)

Materials

- red background paper
- letter patterns on pages 143 and 144 *(optional)*
- white paper and white cardstock
- patterns on pages 34 and 35
- colored markers or crayons
- scissors
- tape or stapler
- brad fastener

Directions

1. Cover the board with red paper.

2. Print out the caption or cut out letters using the letter patterns. Attach the caption to the top of the board.

3. Print the Bible verse on the board or on a strip of paper and attach it to the bottom of the board.

4. Enlarge, color, and cut out all the patterns, using cardstock for the clock hands.

5. Attach the hands of the clock with a brad fastener so they can can be moved.

6. Mount the clock to the center of the board.

7. Mount the pictures around the clock.

8. As you talk about each time pictured, move the hands of the clock to the appropriate time.

Suggested Activities

- Brainstorm with your students some other times to pray (first thing in the morning, when something good happens, when something bad happens, etc.).

- Explain to children that the National Day of Prayer is a special day set aside for everyone in America to pray, especially for our government leaders. Let them suggest specific local, state, and federal leaders to pray for. List any names they know on the board; otherwise, just list the title. Pray together for the leaders listed on the board, asking God to give them wisdom to make the right decisions.

- Have students say this rhyme together.

  Pray today, right away, without delay.
   If you want to obey, pray every day!

Patterns

Patterns

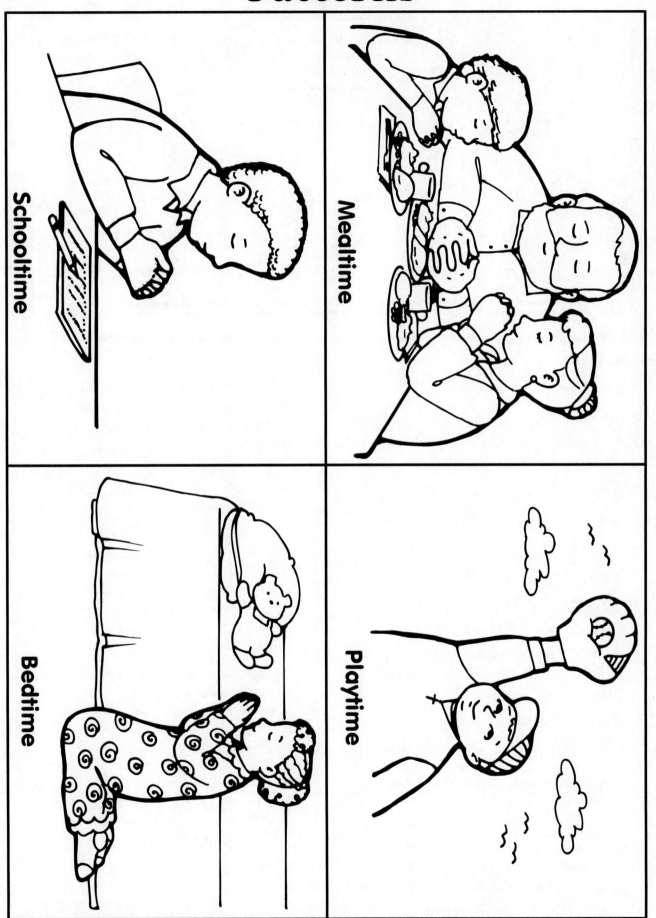

Schooltime

Mealtime

Bedtime

Playtime

**Thank you, God, for moms who care
All the time, everywhere!**

Materials

- pink background paper
- white paper
- letter patterns on pages 143 and 144 (*optional*)
- patterns on pages 37 and 38
- colored markers or crayons
- scissors
- tape or stapler
- photos of children with their mothers

Directions

1. Cover the board with pink paper.

2. Print the rhyming caption at the center of the board or trace the letter patterns on pages 143 and 144.

3. Enlarge, color, and cut out the six pictures of kids and moms.

4. Arrange the pictures on the board. Put the picture of the human mom and children in the middle.

5. Let children add photos of themselves with their moms. If photos are not available, let them draw the pictures.

Suggested Activities

- Talk together about Mother's Day. Let children share what they do to show their love and make their moms feel special on this day.

- Ask students to tell what they know about some Bible moms (such as Eve, Sarah, Rachel, Hannah, and Mary).

- Ask a student to read Isaiah 66:13a aloud. The Bible teaches us that God is like a father, but He is also like a mother to us. How is He like a mother? Let children share how their mothers comfort them when they are sad or sick or hurt. God comforts and cares for us even better than that.

- Reduce the pictures of moms and their babies to about half the size or less. Let students each choose one. Have them color the pictures, then write "I love you" messages on the back. Provide clear adhesive plastic so they can cover the pictures, front and back. Then punch a hole near the top of the picture and let them tie thin ribbon or yarn on it to make a bookmark to give their moms.

Patterns

Patterns

Don't just tell your mom you love her. Show her!

HELP HER

OBEY HER

SHOW RESPECT

LISTEN TO HER

ENJOY HER

PRAY FOR HER

Do not forsake your mother's teaching. (Proverbs 1:8b)

Materials

- light green background paper
- dark blue *(optional)* and white paper
- letter patterns on pages 143 and 144 *(optional)*
- patterns on page 40 and 41
- colored markers or crayons
- tape or stapler
- scissors

Directions

1. Cover the board with light green paper.

2. Print out the caption or cut out letters from dark blue paper using the letter patterns. Attach the caption to the top of the board.

3. Print the Bible verse across the bottom of the board.

4. Enlarge the patterns, color them, and cut them out.

5. Attach the mother pattern to the center of the board with the children on either side.

6. Copy the phrases and attach them to the board.

Suggested Activities

- Discuss ways to show love for our mothers. Let younger children pantomime specific things they can do to show her love. The group can guess what they are doing.

- Teach children this song to sing to their mothers on this special day. Sing the words to the tune of "If You're Happy and You Know It."

You're the best mom in the whole wide world.
You're the best mom in the whole wide world.
I know God gave you to me to help me
be what I should be.
You're the best mom in the whole wide world.

- Print these Bible mothers and their children on the board (without the answers in the parentheses). Let older children match them.

1. Rachel	Moses (6)
2. Sarah	Obed (4)
3. Mary	Joseph (1)
4. Ruth	Jesus (3)
5. Hannah	Isaac (2)
6. Jochabed	Samuel (5)

Pattern

Patterns

A mother is God's gift from above
To show us what it means to love.

These moms deserve the top award,
So bless them in special ways, dear Lord.

Materials

- orange background paper
- white paper
- patterns on page 43 and 44
- colored markers or crayons
- scissors
- glue and tape or stapler
- glitter

Directions

1. Cover the board with orange paper.

2. Print or enlarge the poem on a white paper strip and mount it at the bottom of the board.

3. Enlarge the pattern of the children with the trophy, color it, and cut it out.

4. Add a little glue on the trophy, then sprinkle some glitter on it to make it shine.

5. Mount the pattern to the center of the board.

6. Copy the card patterns and give one to each child.

7. Have children draw pictures of moms (their own or others) and write why they deserve a "Best Mom" award.

8. Scatter the cards all over the board.

Suggested Activities

- Read the poem on the board, then let children read what they wrote on their cards about who should be given a "Best Mom" award.

- Give each student a reduced copy (about half size) of the trophy pattern for a Mother's Day card. Each student can write an "I love you" message on the back and give it to his or her mom or another mom he or she admires.

- Print the word "MOTHER" vertically on the board. Have students come up with words to describe their mothers, each one starting with one of the letters on the board. Some may want to include this on their Mother's Day cards (see above).

- Let students play a game of "Mother, May I?" Stand at one end of the room and be the mother, giving directions to the group, such as the following: "Take three baby steps forward; hop one small hop forward." Students begin at the other end of the room and must say, "Mother, may I?" before every move, or they are out of the game. Those who reach the end of the room first are the winners.

Pattern

Patterns

A mother is God's gift from above   These moms deserve the top award,

To show us what it means to love.   So bless them in special ways, dear Lord.

Materials

- white background paper
- white and brown or black paper
- patterns on pages 46 and 47
- colored markers or crayons
- scissors
- gold or silver star stickers
- tape or stapler

Directions

1. Cover the board with white paper.

2. Copy the sign patterns and cut them out.

3. Cut sign posts from brown or black paper. Assemble the signs and put them on the board as shown.

4. Enlarge the pattern of the patriotic boy, color it, and cut it out.

5. Mount the patriotic boy pattern between the signs.

6. Copy the flag patterns. Give each child a flag to color and cut out, then add to the bulletin board display.

7. Let students put gold or silver star stickers on the bulletin board background.

Suggested Activities

- Ask students if they know people who are in the armed services or served in them in the past. You may want to come prepared with a list of people from your church or town who served their country in the military. Pray together, thanking God for those people. Encourage students to pray aloud for the people by name or to thank God for those who gave their lives.

- Sing "God Bless America" together. Hand out small American flags for children to wave as they sing.

- Let children make additional patriotic flags to take home. Have them write the messages from the signs on the bulletin board on the back of their flags.

- Have students find and read Psalm 33:12 in their Bibles. Ask them if God is the Lord of the United States. In what ways does this nation honor Him? Show them the words, "In God We Trust," on a dollar bill or coin.

Pattern

46

FREEDOM ISN'T FREE!

THANK A SOLDIER AND GOD!

Whoo . . .
makes sure you have freedom to enjoy?

Soldiers fight to keep us free,

To protect our liberty.

Many gave their lives—it's true.

Thank God for them and what they do.

Materials

- green background paper
- white and black paper
- letter patterns on pages 143 and 144 *(optional)*
- patterns on pages 49 and 50
- colored markers or crayons
- tape or stapler
- scissors
- leaves

Directions

1. Cover the board with green paper.

2. Print the question at the top of the board, or cut the letters from black paper using the letter patterns. Attach the question to the board as shown.

3. Copy the owl and poem pattern, enlarging them if necessary.

4. Color them and cut them out.

5. Attach the owl to the left side of the board and the poem to the right side under the question.

6. Attach leaves to the outside border.

Suggested Activities

- Have students read the question on the board aloud. Then let them suggest answers. Choose a student to read the poem to the rest of the group. Discuss how those in the military guard our freedom.

- Sing the poem to the tune of "When Johnny Comes Marching Home Again."

  Soldiers fight to keep us free.
  Hoorah, Hoorah.
  To protect our liberty.
  Hoorah, Hoorah.
  Many give their lives, it's true—
  Thank God for them and what they do
  As they fight to guard our nation's liberty.

- Come prepared with addresses of some soldiers from your church or town printed on envelopes. Hand them out with art paper and crayons or markers so children can create thank-you cards to send them. Encourage children to be creative and come up with their own ideas, or draw the owl and the message on the board on their cards. Make sure children include their names and addresses on the envelopes before you mail them since some may receive responses from soldiers.

Pattern

Pattern

Soldiers fight to keep us free,

To protect our liberty.

Many gave their lives—it's true.

Thank God for them and what they do.

I pledge allegiance to the flag of the
United States of America.

One nation under God.

Materials

- red, white, and blue background paper
- gold star stickers
- white paper
- letter patterns on pages 143 and 144 *(optional)*
- patterns on pages 52–54
- colored markers or crayons
- tape or stapler
- scissors

Directions

1. Cover the board with red and white paper stripes and star stickers on a blue square for a large American flag. Or, make multiple copies of the flag pattern on page 52. Color and cut them out. Attach the flags to the board.

2. Print the caption at the top and bottom of the board or use the letter patterns on pages 143 and 144.

3. Copy the four children patterns, enlarging them as necessary. Color them and cut them out.

4. Attach the children in the middle of the board.

Suggested Activities

- Lead children in saying the Pledge of Allegiance to the flag. Talk about it to make sure they understand what it means. Explain that to pledge allegiance means to promise your loyalty. Discuss the meaning of the following words: republic (nation governed by citizens' votes), indivisible (not able to be divided or split up), liberty (freedom), justice (fairness).

- Do students know what the flag's 13 stripes represent? *(the 13 original colonies)* How many stars are on the flag? *(50)* What do they represent? *(the current 50 states)* Challenge students to think of 13 ways God has blessed the United States, one for every stripe on the flag.

- Talk about how we show respect for our flag (stand up, take off our hats, put our hands on our hearts or salute, don't talk, hold it, or fly it so it does not touch the ground).

- Ask volunteer students to pray aloud, thanking God for all that the American flag represents to us (a beautiful land of freedom and opportunity).

Pattern

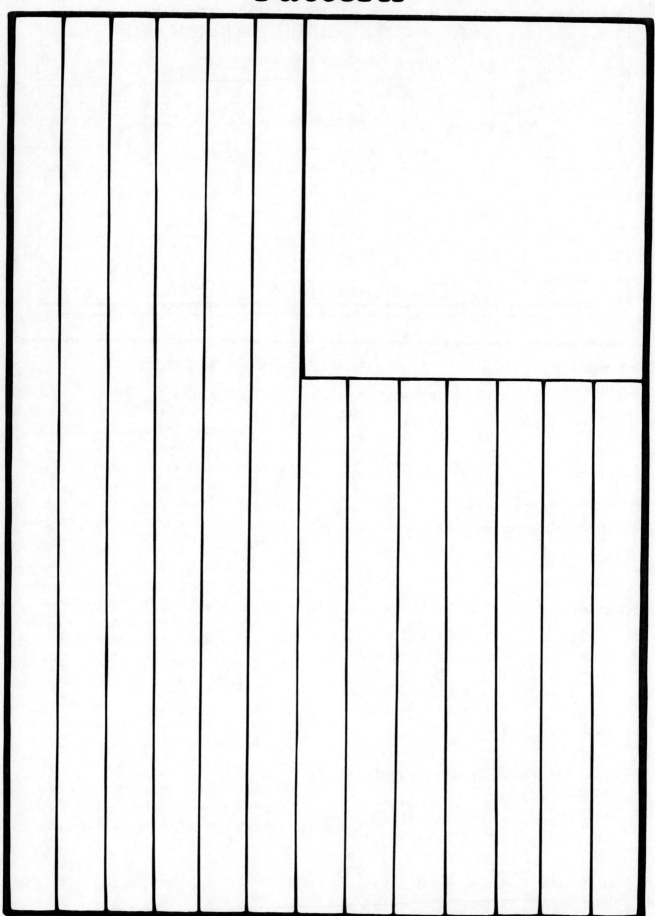

Patterns

Patterns

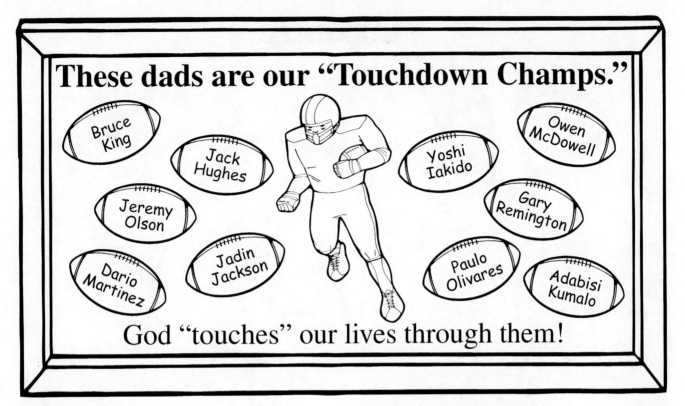

Materials

- yellow background paper
- white and light brown paper
- letter patterns on pages 143 and 144 (optional)
- patterns on pages 56 and 57
- colored markers or crayons
- tape or stapler
- scissors

Directions

1. Cover the board with yellow paper.

2. Print the caption or use the letters patterns. Attach the caption to the top and bottom as shown.

3. Enlarge the football player pattern.

4. Color the pattern and cut it out.

5. Attach the football player to the center of the board.

6. Copy the football patterns on light brown paper and give one to each student to cut out.

7. Have students write their dads' names on the footballs, then mount them on the board.

Suggested Activities

- Have a volunteer read the statements on the board. Then ask students to share specific ways their dads have "touched" their lives.

- Give each student two enlarged copies of the football and a reduced copy of the football player. Help them staple the two football patterns together at the top to make a card. They can color the football player and glue it to the front of the card; then write a Father's Day message inside. Make sure they all sign their names to their cards.

- Provide older students with Bibles that have concordances in the back. Challenge them to find Bible verses about fathers. Let them read their verses aloud. Discuss what the verses teach us about what fathers should do and how God is a father to us.

- Brainstorm other names for "father" (dad, pop, daddy, pappa, etc.). Print the names on the board. Then ask children which names they use. Which is the most popular?

- Pray together, thanking God our Father for giving us fathers.

Pattern

Patterns

Hop to it! Give Dad a Happy Father's Day!

Wise children bring joy to their father. (see Proverbs 10:1)

Materials

- blue background paper
- white and green paper
- short, thin strip of cardstock
- letter patterns on pages 143 and 144 (optional)
- patterns on page 59 and 60
- colored markers or crayons
- tape or stapler
- scissors
- glue

Directions

1. Cover the board with blue paper.

2. Use the letters patterns to cut out the words for the caption from green paper or print them on the board as shown.

3. Print the Bible verse on a strip of green paper and attach it at the bottom of the board.

4. Enlarge the big frog pattern and copy the lily pad on green paper.

5. Color the big frog.

6. Attach the big lily pad to the center of the board.

7. Accordion fold a short strip of cardstock and glue one end to the back of the frog.

8. Attach the other end to the board so the frog moves a little on the lily pad.

9. Copy the small frog patterns and give one to each student.

10. Have students write on the lily pads what they will do or say to give their dads a "hoppy" Father's Day.

11. Scatter the small frogs all over the board.

Suggested Activities

- Read the Bible verse on the board. Then ask children to suggest ways they can be wise and bring joy to their fathers (obey, make wise choices, love God, etc.).

- Teach children this song to the tune of "I've Got the Joy, Joy, Joy, Joy Down in My Heart." Let them make up their own words to the last line and sing it for their dads.

I will bring joy, joy, joy, joy, joy to my dad,
Joy to my dad, joy to my dad.
I will bring joy, joy, joy, joy, joy to my dad.
I'll do what he tells me.

Patterns

Patterns

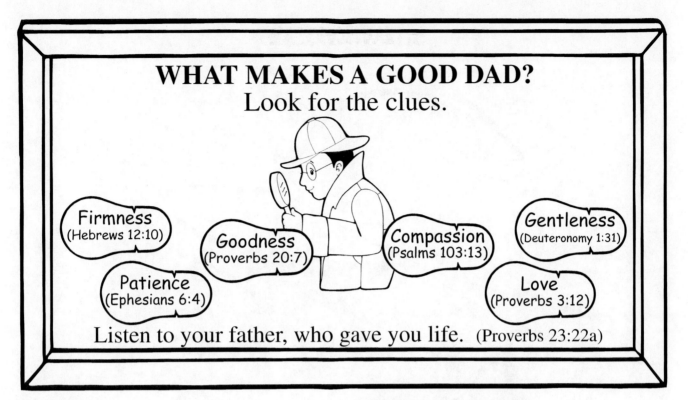

WHAT MAKES A GOOD DAD?
Look for the clues.

Firmness
(Hebrews 12:10)

Goodness
(Proverbs 20:7)

Patience
(Ephesians 6:4)

Compassion
(Psalms 103:13)

Gentleness
(Deuteronomy 1:31)

Love
(Proverbs 3:12)

Listen to your father, who gave you life. (Proverbs 23:22a)

Materials

- light green background paper
- white paper and black paper *(optional)*
- letter patterns on pages 143 and 144 *(optional)*
- patterns on pages 62 and 63
- colored markers or crayons
- tape or stapler
- scissors
- magnifying glass *(optional)*

Directions

1. Cover the board with light green paper.
2. Cut out the letter patterns from black paper for the caption or print it on the board.
3. Print the Bible verse at the bottom of the board.
4. Enlarge the detective pattern, color it, cut it out, and attach it to the center of the board.
5. Copy the footprints and write the character trait and verse on them. Color them, and cut them out. Scatter the footprints around the detective.
6. If possible, attach a real magnifying glass to the board.

Suggested Activities

- Have students look up and read the Bible verses featured on the board to discover for themselves what God's Word says about fathers. Call on volunteers to read the verses aloud.
- Play a game of "Bible Dads and Their Kids." Print the following names on the board in two columns (without the answers in parentheses). Have children match the child with his father.

  1. Adam   Joseph (3)
  2. Noah   Joshua (4)
  3. Jacob   Abel (1)
  4. Nun   Shem (2)
  5. David   John (6)
  6. Zebedee   Solomon (5)

- Let children draw pictures of their dads (or Bible dads if they do not have dads). Then they can hold up their pictures and talk about them.

Pattern

Patterns

Firmness
(Hebrews 12:10)

Patience
(Ephesians 6:4)

Goodness
(Proverbs 20:7)

Compassion
(Psalms 103:13)

Gentleness
(Deuteronomy 1:31)

Love
(Proverbs 3:12)

Materials

- light blue background paper
- white paper
- patterns on pages 65 and 66
- letter patterns on pages 143 and 144 *(optional)*
- scissors
- tape or stapler
- colored markers
- two small American flags

Directions

1. Cover the board with light blue paper.

2. Print out the caption or cut out letters using the letter patterns. Attach the caption across the top of the board.

3. Enlarge the United States pattern, cut it out, and mount it on the board.

4. Enlarge the children patterns. Make enough copies so they stretch across the center of the board. Color them and cut them out. Mount them on the board as shown.

5. Give each student a copy of the house pattern to color and cut out, then write his or her name in the middle. Scatter the houses all over the board.

6. Attach the small American flags to the hands of the children located on the ends of the bulletin board.

Suggested Activities

- Sing "God Bless America" together. Then ask them to share ways they think God has blessed the United States.

- Provide red, white, and blue yarn. Let students draw American flags on white cardstock, then glue yarn over them. Provide glue and glitter for students to add stars to their flags. Help them add dots of glue and carefully place glitter on just the dots.

- Make extra copies of the houses for kids to color. Instead of having them write their names on them, have them write how God has blessed them.

Pattern

Patterns

66

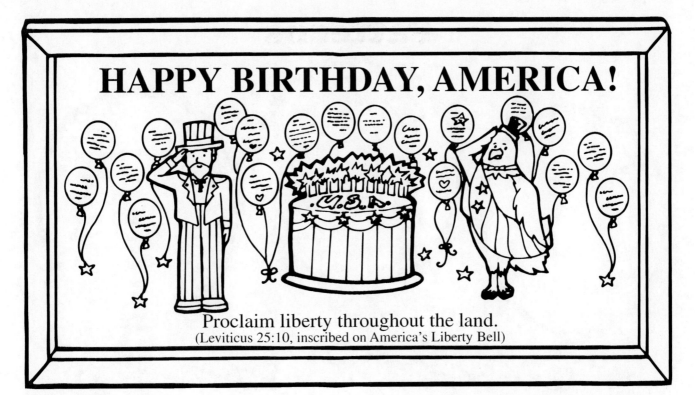

HAPPY BIRTHDAY, AMERICA!

Proclaim liberty throughout the land.
(Leviticus 25:10, inscribed on America's Liberty Bell)

Materials

- red background paper
- blue and white paper
- patterns on pages 68 and 69
- letter patterns on pages 143 and 144 *(optional)*
- scissors
- tape or stapler
- colored markers
- colored ribbons

Directions

1. Cover the board with red paper.

2. Print out the caption or cut out letters for the from blue paper using the letter patterns. Attach the caption across the top of the board.

3. Enlarge the patterns, color them, and cut them out.

4. Mount the cake at the center of the board.

5. Mount the Uncle Sam pattern on one side of the cake and the eagle on the other side.

6. Give each student a copy of the balloon pattern.

7. Have students write "thank you" prayers to God for America on the balloons, then scatter them all over the board.

8. Attach colored ribbons to the balloons.

9. Cut stars out of blue or white paper and attach them to the board.

Suggested Activities

- Explain to the children that the eagle is the official national bird of the United States. Uncle Sam is also a national symbol. Ask them to suggest other national symbols (flag, Liberty Bell, etc.). Ask if the Bible could be one of our national symbols. Why or why not?

- Older students can write haiku poems about America. Haiku poems have only three lines. The first and third lines contain five syllables and the second line contains seven syllables. Here is an example:

  Thank God for freedom,
  Liberty for everyone
  In America!

- Pray together, encouraging children to repeat the prayers they wrote and put on the board.

Patterns

Patterns

Materials

- blue background paper
- red and white paper
- patterns on pages 71 and 72
- letter patterns on pages 143 and 144 *(optional)*
- scissors
- tape or stapler
- colored markers
- glue *(optional)*

Directions

1. Cover the board with blue paper.

2. Print out the caption or cut out letters from red paper, using the letter patterns. Attach the caption across the top of the board.

3. Enlarge the USA patterns on red paper and cut them out. Mount them to the board as shown.

4. Copy the rhyme on white paper and cut it out. Mount it at the bottom of the board.

5. Copy the star patterns, one for each student, on white paper and cut them out (or let students cut them out).

6. Have students glue photos of themselves on the stars (or draw pictures of themselves on them) and attach them to the USA letters.

7. Attach a white star to each corner of the board.

Suggested Activities

- Ask students to share why they are proud to be Americans.

- Make extra copies of the stars on red or white paper. Give each child five or six stars. Help them staple the stars together to make star-shaped books. They can write for what freedoms they are thankful on the star pages. When they are done with their books, have them pass them around so everyone can see everyone else's.

- Pray together, encouraging children to thank God for the things they love about America.

- Let students make patriotic bookmarks. Hand out cardstock strips, about 2" x 6" (5 cm x 15 cm), on which you have printed the rhyme from the bulletin board. Let them color the strips red, white, and blue, and stick gummed stars on them. Provide clear adhesive plastic so they can cover their bookmarks to protect them.

Patterns

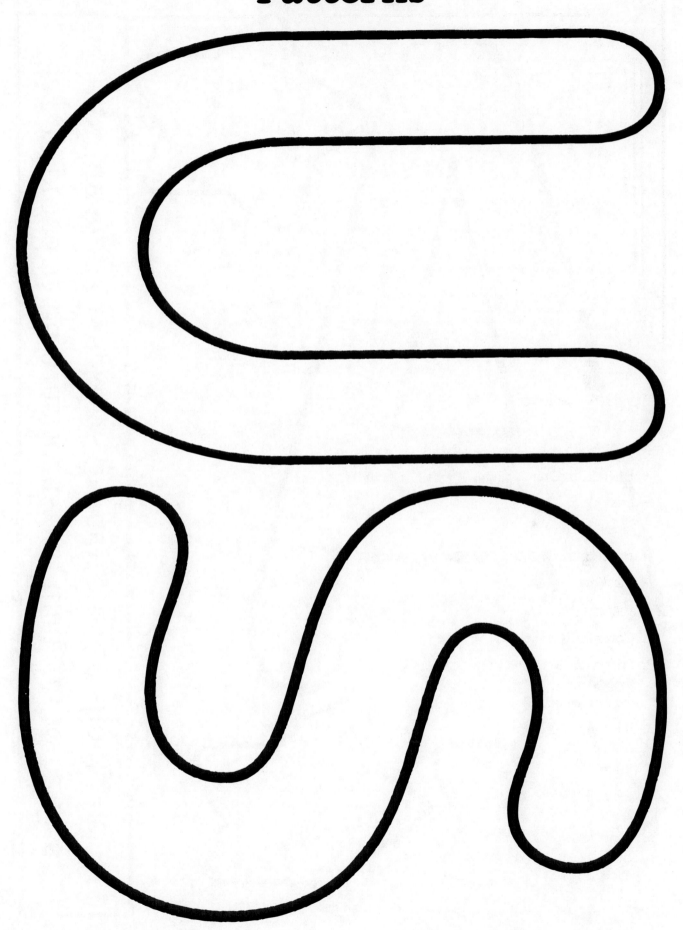

Patterns

We're proud to be Americans and thankful to be free,
Asking God to make us the citizens we should be.

72

TIME WITH GRANDPARENTS

CHOO-CHOO-CHOOSE

GRANDPARENTS EXPRESS

How has God used your grandparents to bless you?

Materials

- medium blue background paper
- white and black paper *(optional)*
- patterns on pages 74 and 75
- letter patterns on pages 143 and 144 *(optional)*
- scissors
- colored markers
- tape or stapler

Directions

1. Cover the board with medium blue paper.

2. Print out the caption or cut out letters from black paper, using the letter patterns. Attach the caption across the top of the board in white smoke puff shapes as shown.

3. Cut out a few small white puff shapes and attach them above the smoke stack, leading up to the caption.

4. Print the question at the bottom of the board.

5. Enlarge the train patterns, color them, and cut them out.

6. Attach them to the board.

Suggested Activities

- Let children share how God has used their grandparents to bless them.

- Play a game of "Guess Whose Grandparent?" Have each child write down something about his or her grandparents or whisper it in your ear so you can write it down. (Example: My grandpa fought in the army in Vietnam.) Then read each one aloud and see if students can guess whose grandparent you are reading about. Then pray together, encouraging each child to thank God for his or her grandparents.

- Invite children's grandparents to come to a Grandparents' Day celebration. Let the children say Bible verses they have memorized, sing songs, and serve punch and cookies to their grandparents. Those who do not have grandparents living nearby can "adopt" some for the occasion.

- Let children design cards for their grandparents to express their love and appreciation for them. Print this Bible verse on the board for them to include in the cards: "I have not stopped giving thanks for you, remembering you in my prayers." (Ephesians 1:16)

Pattern

Pattern

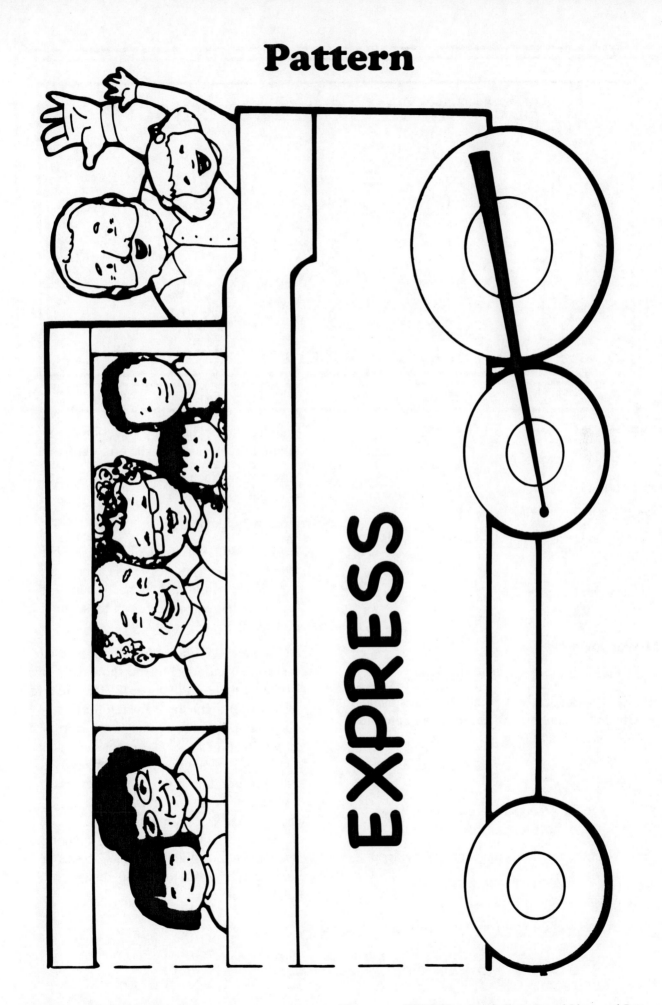

EXPRESS

Celebrate Grandparents!

Grandparents are a special treat from God.

Materials

- lavender background paper
- white paper
- patterns on pages 77 and 78
- letter patterns on pages 143 and 144 (optional)
- scissors
- tape or stapler
- colored markers, including purple

Directions

1. Cover the board with lavender paper.

2. Print out the caption or cut out letters using the letter patterns. Attach the caption to the top of the board.

3. Print the statement across the bottom of the board.

4. Enlarge the grandparents and child picture, color it, and cut it out.

5. Mount the picture at the center of the board.

6. Copy the ice-cream cones, one for each child, and hand them out.

7. Have each child write on the cone about a good time he or she has had with grandparents. Then they can color the ice cream to represent their favorite flavors.

8. Have them attach their ice-cream cones all over the board.

Suggested Activities

- Let each child share what is on his or her ice-cream cone, adding details about the experience with grandparents. Then pray together, thanking God for all those good times with grandparents.

- Ask students to brainstorm things they can do for their grandparents to show their love. List their ideas on the board. Here are a few ideas to get them started: pray for them, obey them, carry things for them, help them do yardwork, etc. Then give each student a copy of the ice-cream cone pattern. Have each print on the front of the ice-cream cone "A Special Treat for You." On the back, each student can print what he or she will do for the grandparents, making it a coupon that can be redeemed any time. The coupon cones can be given to grandparents to celebrate the day.

Pattern

Patterns

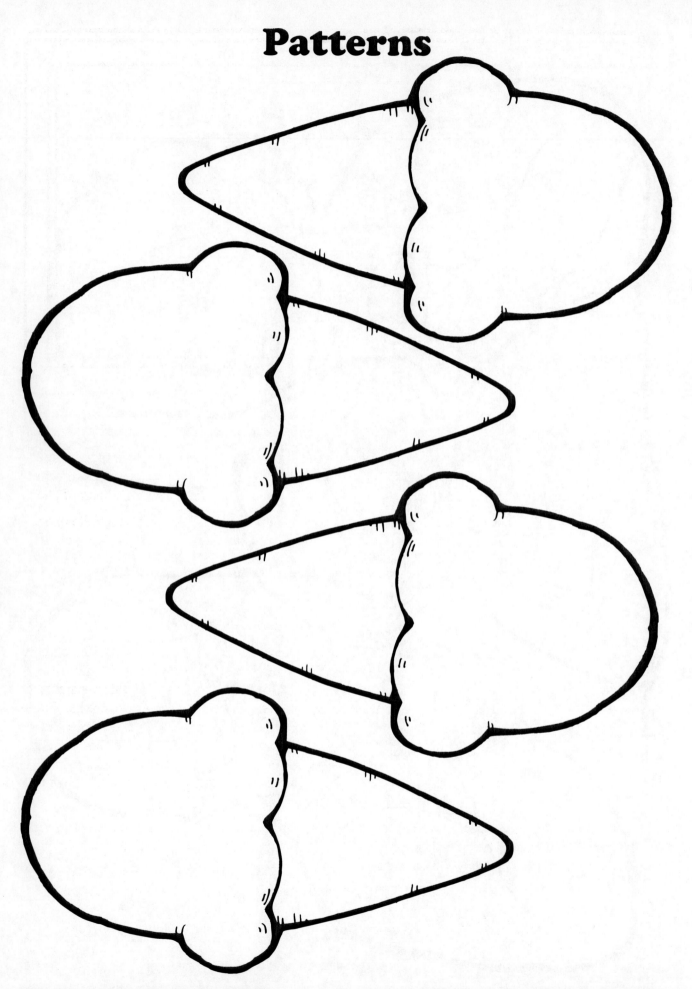

Here's a very smart thing to do: **Listen to grandparents and learn something new!**

Before you set up this board, have students record several grandparents telling stories or talking to children.

Materials

- yellow background paper
- white paper
- patterns on page 80
- letter patterns on pages 143 and 144 *(optional)*
- cassette/CD player
- scissors
- tape or stapler
- colored markers, including black
- photos or drawings of themselves and/or grandparents

Directions

1. Cover the board with yellow paper.

2. Print the rhyme in large letters on a sheet of white paper or cut out letters using the letter patterns and mount the rhyme at the center of the board.

3. Enlarge the patterns of the grandmother and grandfather, color them, and cut them out.

4. Mount the grandmother on one side of the rhyme and the grandfather on the other side.

5. Have children attach photos or drawings of themselves and/or grandparents to the board all around the grandmother and grandfather.

6. Place a cassette/CD player on a table under the board. Put the tape of grandparents talking in it. Children can listen to the cassette/CD as they look at the bulletin board.

Suggested Activities

- Ask a volunteer to read James 1:19 aloud. Talk about the importance of listening, especially to those who are older: parents, teachers, the pastor, and grandparents. Point out that God gave each of us two ears and one mouth, so He must have meant for us to listen more than we talk. Ask students to tell about things they have learned while listening to their grandparents talk.

- Say this rap together. Children can learn it to say for their grandparents.

   Grandparents are very nice;
   They help us and give good advice.
   Listening to what they say
   Is interesting, and it's God's way!

Patterns

When you go to school, remember,

SCHOOL

God goes with you!

Joshua 1:9 TAKE ONE

Materials

- green background paper
- white paper
- patterns on pages 82 and 83
- letter patterns on pages 143 and 144 *(optional)*
- scissors
- colored markers, including black
- envelope
- tape and stapler

Directions

1. Cover the board with green paper.

2. Print out the caption or cut out letters using the letter patterns. Attach the caption to the top and bottom of the board.

3. Enlarge the two school bus patterns, color them, and cut them out. Tape them together to make a big bus.

4. Mount the bus at the center of the board.

5. Use black marker to draw exhaust clouds behind the bus. Or, cut out exhaust clouds from white paper and attach them behind the bus.

6. Copy the Bible verse card, one for every student.

7. Cut an envelope in half. Print on it, "Joshua 1:9 TAKE ONE."

8. Attach the envelope to the bottom corner of the board. Place the Bible verse cards in the envelope for students to take.

Suggested Activities

- Read Joshua 1:9 aloud. Ask students when God is with them. *(all the time)* Where is He with them? *(everywhere)* They can count on God to be with them and help them at school. They can talk to Him anytime by silently praying in their thoughts without even closing their eyes. Encourage students to take the Bible verse cards to school with them to keep in their desks or notebooks.

- Let students share prayer requests related to the new school year. Write them on the board; then let them volunteer to pray aloud for one another's requests. End the prayer time by thanking God for going with each student to school every day.

- Have a Bible drill with older students competing to look up these Bible verses that promise God's presence: Exodus 33:14; Psalm 145:18; Hebrews 13:5b; Jeremiah 1:8; Deuteronomy 31:6; Psalm 139:7–10.

Patterns

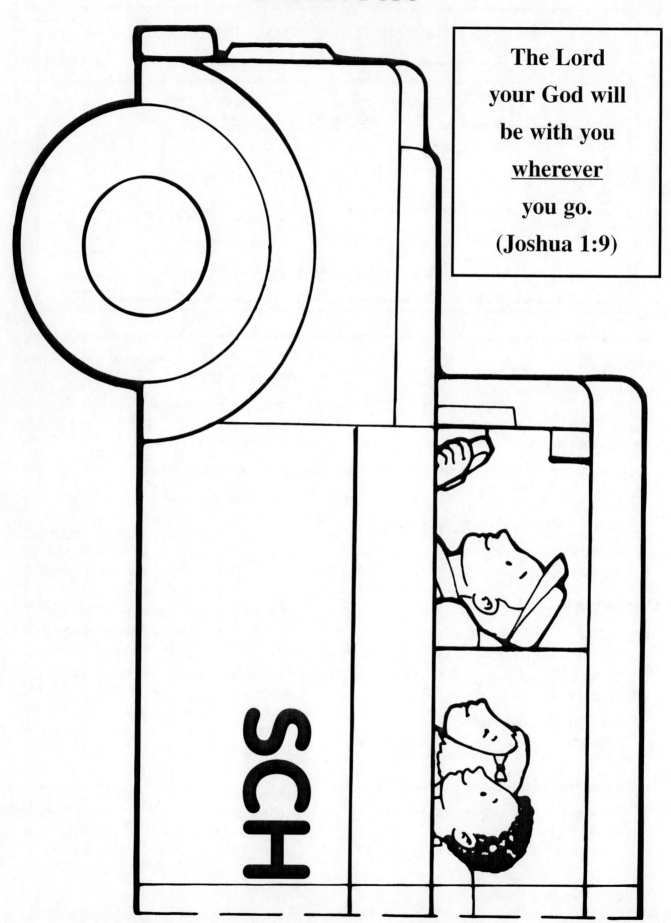

The Lord your God will be with you <u>wherever</u> you go. (Joshua 1:9)

SCH

Pattern

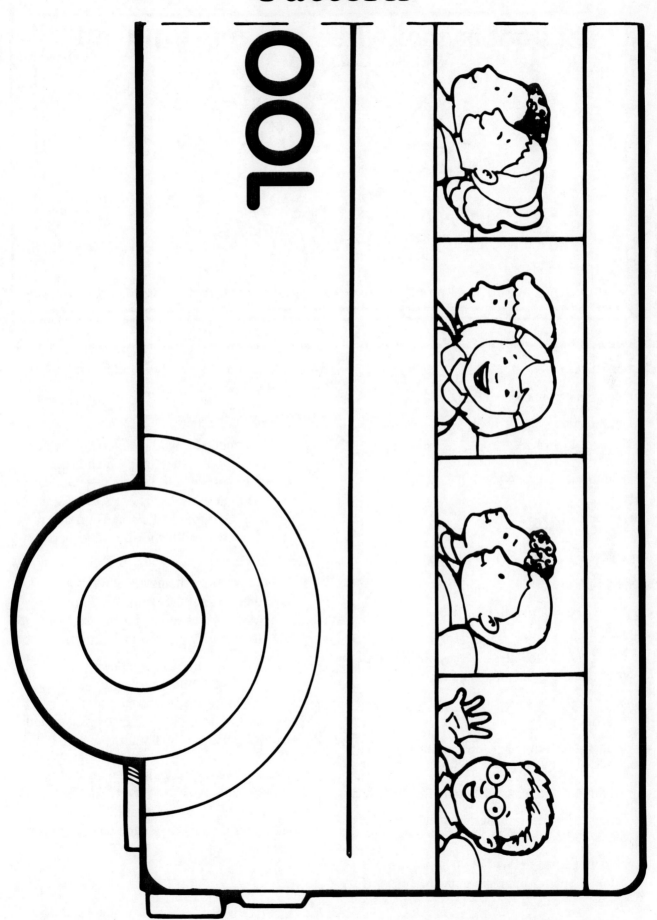

School is cool when you trust in God!

I can do everything through him who gives me strength. (Philippians 4:13)

Materials

- blue background paper
- white paper
- letter patterns on pages 143 and 144 (optional)
- patterns on pages 85 and 86
- scissors
- tape or stapler
- colored markers

Directions

1. Cover the board with blue paper.

2. Print the caption or cut letters from white paper, using the letter patterns. Mount the caption across the top of the board.

3. Print the Bible verse at the bottom of the board.

4. Enlarge the octopus pattern, color it, and cut it out.

5. Mount the octopus at the center of the board.

6. Enlarge the school materials patterns, color them, and cut them out.

7. Attach the materials to the octopus' arms. You may prefer to create your own school materials or use real ones for the octopus to

hold that more closely correlate with what your students are studying.

Suggested Activities

- Ask volunteers to tell how God has helped them at school. Then let each child share what he or she would like to have God help them with at school. Pray together, some thanking God for His help and and others asking for help with specific subjects or activities.

- To help children memorize Philippians 4:13, have them repeat the words after you. Say it together as a cheer as the children jump, raise their arms, and do other actions.

  I can do (I can do)
  Everything (everything)
  Through him (through him)
  Who gives me strength (who gives me strength).
  Philippians 4:13 (Philippians 4:13)

- Give each student a reduced copy of the octopus pattern. Have them write the bulletin board caption on it (School is cool when you trust in God!) and take it home for a reminder.

Pattern

Patterns

Tell what God has done for you.

Don't keep it under your hat!

Materials

- orange background paper
- white paper/black paper *(optional)*
- letter patterns on pages 143 and 144 *(optional)*
- patterns on pages 88 and 89
- scissors
- tape or stapler
- colored markers
- pens or fine-tip markers

Directions

1. Cover the board with orange paper.

2. Print out the caption or cut letters from black paper, using the letter patterns. Mount the caption on the board as shown.

3. Copy the Pilgrim boy pattern, color it, and cut it out. Cut out the Pilgrim hat and Bible verse rectangle separately.

4. Mount the Pilgrim boy at the center of the board.

5. Tape or staple the boy's hat over the Bible verse and attach it to the head of the Pilgrim boy at the top only so the hat can be lifted up to reveal the verse under it.

6. Copy the Pilgrim hat shapes and give one to each child. Have them write on the hats what God has done for them, then scatter them over the board.

Suggested Activities

- Explain to your children that "keeping something under your hat" is an expression that means hiding something or keeping quiet about it. That is definitely not what God wants us to do when it come to His work in our lives.

- Conduct a Bible drill, letting older students see how quickly they can find these "thankful" verses in their Bibles: Philippians 4:6; 1 Chronicles 16:8; Colossians 3:15; Psalm 100:4; 1 Thessalonians 5:18; 2 Corinthians 9:15.

- Let children tell what God has done for them, adding more detail to what is on the board. Then pray together, encouraging them to express their thanks to God.

Patterns

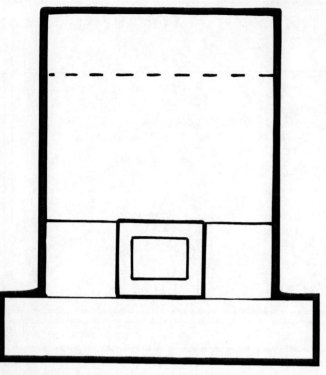

I will sing of the Lord's great love forever.

(Psalm 89:1a)

Patterns

Thank You, God!

You satisfy the thirsty and fill the hungry with good things.
(see Psalm 107:9)

Materials

- green background paper
- white paper
- letter patterns on pages 143 and 144 (*optional*)
- patterns on pages 91 and 92
- scissors
- colored markers
- tape or stapler
- magazines that can be cut

Directions

1. Cover the board with green paper.

2. Print the caption or cut letters from white paper, using the letter patterns. Mount the caption at the top of the board.

3. Print out the verse on the bottom of the board.

4. Enlarge the five patterns, color them, and cut them out.

5. Mount the picture of people eating dinner at the center of the board. Attach the animal pictures around it.

6. Let children cut pictures of foods they like from magazines and scatter them over the board or have children write what food or drink for which they are thankful.

Suggested Activities

- Read Psalm 104:10–28 together. Talk about how God cares for all the creatures and people He made. Let children tell what they know about how birds and animals find their food. Remind them that even though their parents buy their food in stores, it is God who makes it grow and ripen, and gives them money to buy the food they eat every day.

- Provide nature, gardening, and wildlife magazines from which children may cut pictures to make collages to illustrate God's care of His creation. They can draw pictures of themselves on the collages to show that God provides for them too. Have them print the bulletin board Bible verse, Psalm 107:9, on their collages.

- Challenge older students to use Bibles with concordances to find other Bible verses about how God provides our needs. They can use key words such as the following: *provides, provider, satisfy, satisfies,* and *needs.* Ask them to read the verses aloud for the rest of the group.

Pattern

Patterns

92

Give thanks to the Lord, for he is good; his love endures forever. (Psalm 106:1)

This is the day the Lord has made; let us rejoice and be glad in it. (Psalm 118:24)

The Lord has done great things for us, and we are filled with joy. (Psalm 126:3)

I praise you because I am fearfully and wonderfully made. (Psalm 139:14a)

Lord, we lift Your name on high to praise You and thank You.

Materials

- blue background paper
- white paper
- patterns on pages 94 and 95
- letter patterns on pages 143 and 144 *(optional)*
- scissors
- colored markers
- cotton balls
- tape or stapler
- glue

Directions

1. Cover the board with blue paper.

2. Print the caption or cut out letters using the letter patterns. Attach to the bottom of the board.

3. Enlarge the balloon pattern and make four copies of it. Color each one differently and cut them out.

4. Copy the Bible verses and glue them on the balloons.

5. Mount the balloons on the board.

6. Cut cloud shapes from white paper. Glue cotton balls on them and add them to the board.

Suggested Activities

- Sing the praise chorus "Lord, We Lift Your Name on High." Explain that "lifting God's name on high" means praising Him. Sing other praise songs together as time allows.

- Call on volunteers to read the Bible verses on the board aloud. Ask students to tell other reasons to praise God.

- Give each student a reduced copy of the hot air balloon to color and cut out. They can glue the balloon on the front of a sheet of folded paper to make a Thanksgiving card. Let each one choose one of the Bible verses from the board to print on the card. Then the student can write a Thanksgiving message on the inside of the card to give to a friend or relative.

- Let each child choose a partner with whom to pray. Encourage the pairs to praise God for the reasons mentioned earlier as they sit together and pray quietly.

Pattern

Patterns

Give thanks to the Lord, for he is good; his love endures forever. **(Psalm 106:1)**	**The Lord has done great things for us, and we are filled with joy.** **(Psalm 126:3)**
This is the day the Lord has made; let us rejoice and be glad in it. **(Psalm 118:24)**	**I praise you because I am fearfully and wonderfully made.** **(Psalm 139:14a)**

It's very clear,

This time of year is all about . . .

JESUS

She will give birth to a son, and you are to give him the name Jesus, because he will save his people from their sins. (Matthew 1:21)

Materials

- white background paper
- white paper and paper of Christmas colors
- letter patterns on pages 143 and 144 (*optional*)
- patterns on pages 97 and 98
- scissors
- tape or stapler
- colored markers
- artificial holly or Christmas garland

Directions

1. Cover the board with white paper.

2. Print out the caption or cut letters from red paper using the letter patterns. Attach them to the board as shown.

3. Carefully print "JESUS" across the board in letters as large as possible or use the letter patterns to help you.

4. Print the Bible verse across the bottom of the board.

5. Make multiple copies of the ornament patterns on page 98 on Christmas colored paper and cut them out.

7. Outline the "JESUS" letters with the ornaments any way you choose.

8. Enlarge the pattern on page 97, color it, and cut it out.

9. Attach the pattern of the child on the right of the board as if decorating the letters.

10. Attach artificial holly or Christmas garland around the edge of the bulletin board for a festive border.

Suggested Activities

- Cut a large Christmas tree shape from green paper and mount it on a wall. Make copies of the ornament patterns for children to color and cut out to decorate the tree. Explain that Christmas trees are evergreens, which means they are green year 'round, like Jesus' love for us which is always the same.

- Challenge students to make up new words about Jesus' birth to the tune of "We Wish You a Merry Christmas" and sing them. (Example: God sent down His Son to save us, God sent down His Son to save us, God sent down His Son to save us and show us His love.)

96

Pattern

Patterns

Materials

- black background paper
- white and yellow paper
- letter patterns on pages 143 and 144 (optional)
- patterns on pages 100 and 101
- scissors
- colored markers
- tape or stapler
- strings of tiny white Christmas lights

Directions

1. Cover the board with black paper.

2. Print the caption or cut the letters from yellow paper using the letter patterns. Attach the caption to the board as shown.

3. Enlarge the patterns, color them, and cut them out.

4. Put the picture of Jesus at the center of the board with one child on each side.

5. Attach tiny lights for a border around the bulletin board and around the picture of Jesus.

Suggested Activities

- Choose students to read the Bible verses on the board aloud. Ask them if they know any other Bible verses about Jesus as the light. Challenge older students to use Bibles with concordances to find other "light" Bible verses and read them to the group.

- Turn off the lights in the room and cover any windows to make the room fairly dark. Explain that the Bible says that the world is in darkness, which means that people's sin makes the world a dark place to live. But God sent Jesus into the world to bring His light (turn on a flashlight) and forgiveness to us. Pray together, encouraging children to thank God for giving us His light.

- Sing these words to the tune of "B-I-N-G-O."

Jesus came into the world to be the light of God.
L-I-G-H-T, L-I-G-H-T, L-I-G-H-T,
He was the light of God.

- Give students copies of the "light" Bible verses on the board and encourage them to memorize them.

Pattern

Patterns

Arise, shine, for your light has come. (Isaiah 60:1a)

Jesus said, "I am the light of the world." (John 8:12a)

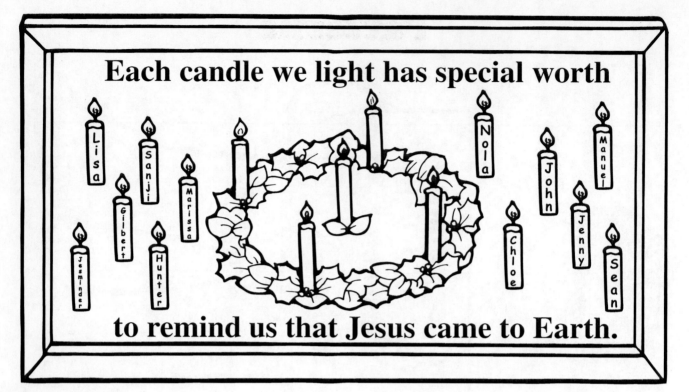

Each candle we light has special worth

to remind us that Jesus came to Earth.

Materials

- blue background paper
- white paper
- patterns on page 103
- letter patterns on pages 143 and 144 *(optional)*
- scissors
- colored markers (including green, purple, pink, and yellow)
- tape or stapler

Directions

1. Cover the board with blue paper.

2. Print the caption at the top and bottom of the board as shown or use the letter patterns to help you.

3. Enlarge the patterns. Make five copies of the large candles and flames and multiple copies of the leaves.

4. Color the leaves various shades of green and cut them out.

5. Color three of the large candles purple, one pink, and leave one white. Color all the flames yellow.

6. Arrange the green leaves in a large wreath circle at the center of the board. Place the

four colored candles evenly spaced in the wreath. Place the white candle in the center.

7. Each week of Advent, choose someone to "light" a candle by attaching a colored flame to the top of it. (The purple candles should be lit the first two weeks, then the pink one, then the other purple one. The white candle is lit on Christmas Eve.)

8. Copy the small candles, one for each child. Have them color and cut out their candles, then write their names on them and add them to the bulletin board display.

Suggested Activities

- Talk about what the Advent wreath and candles mean. Advent, which begins on the Sunday closest to November 30 and goes until Christmas, is a time of looking forward to Jesus' coming. The green Advent wreath represents the eternal life we have in Jesus. The candles remind us that He is the light of the world. The first candle stands for hope, the second for peace, the third for joy, and the fourth for love. The white candle, called the Christ candle, reminds us that we can have hope, peace, joy, and love only in Jesus Christ. Pray together, encouraging children to thank God for sending Jesus to the earth.

Patterns

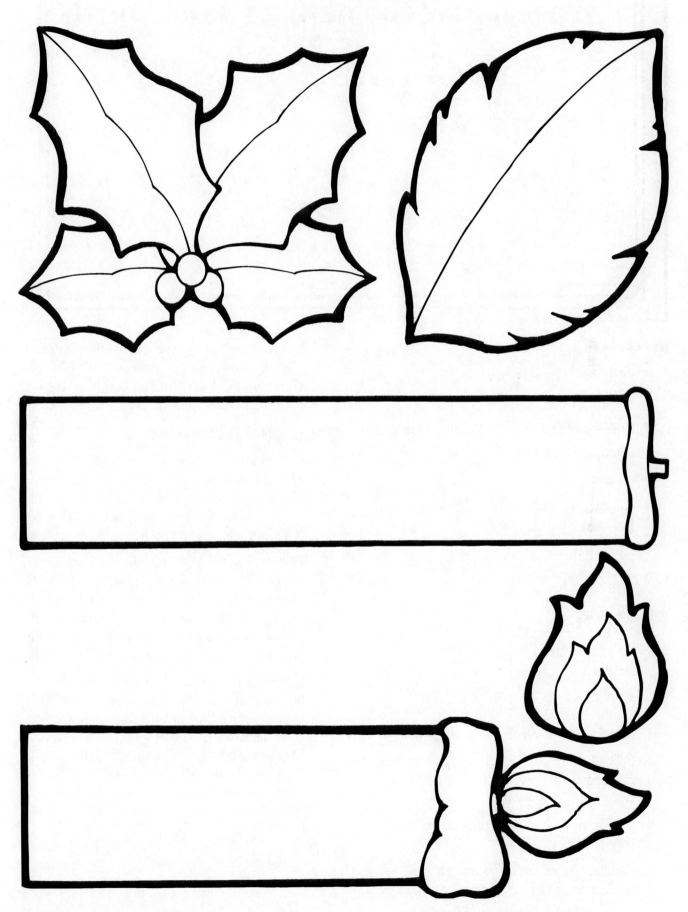

Angels gave the news of Jesus' birth

The angel said, "Today in the town of David a Savior has been born to you."
(see Luke 2:11)

Materials

- white background paper
- white paper/red paper *(optional)*
- letter patterns on pages 143 and 144 *(optional)*
- patterns on pages 105 and 106
- scissors
- tape or stapler
- colored markers
- glue
- gold and silver glitter

Directions

1. Cover the board with white paper.

2. Print out the caption or cut letters from red paper using the letter patterns. Attach the caption to the top of the board as shown.

3. Print the Bible verse across the bottom of the board.

4. Enlarge the patterns of the boy and girl, color them, and cut them out.

5. Mount the boy and girl patterns on the board.

6. Copy the small angel pattern for each student.

7. Let students cut out the angels, then spread glue on them, and cover them with gold or silver glitter. Let them add their angels to the board around the caption.

Suggested Activities

- Let students tell the story of the angels giving Jesus' birth announcement to shepherds (Luke 2:8-16) in their own words. Ask them to imagine how they would have felt if they had seen and heard the angels.

- Copy the small angel on cardstock for each child. Let them color and cut out the angels to make Christmas tree ornaments. Let them add glitter to them as they did for their bulletin board angels. Provide thin ribbon or yarn so they can put hangers on their angels.

- Have older students read in their Bibles how angels were involved in other facets of Jesus' birth: an angel spoke to Mary—Luke 1:26–37; an angel spoke to Joseph—Matthew 1:18–21; an angel warned Joseph to go to Egypt—Matthew 2:13–15; an angel told Joseph to go back home—Matthew 2:19–21.

- Sing the Christmas carol "Angels We Have Heard on High."

Pattern

Patterns

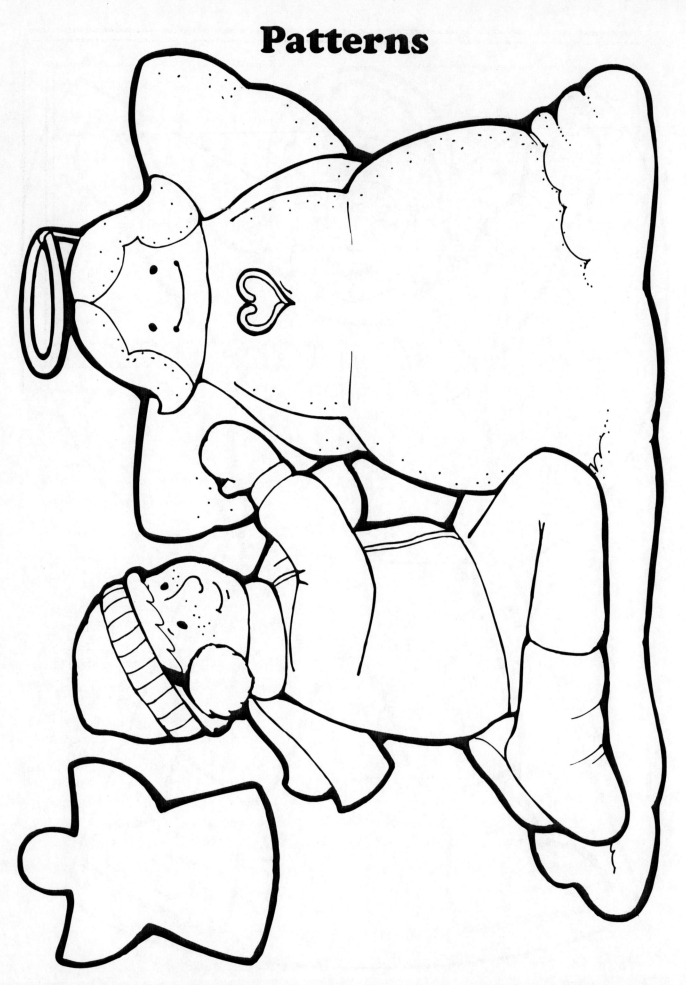

Jesus—"The Way" in a Manger

Jesus said, "I am the way and the truth and the life. No one comes to the Father except through me." (John 14:6)

Materials

- dark blue background paper
- white and gold or yellow paper
- letter patterns on pages 143 and 144 *(optional)*
- patterns on pages 108 and 109
- scissors
- tape or stapler
- colored markers
- real straw or hay *(optional)*

Directions

1. Cover the board with dark blue paper.

2. Print the caption or cut letters from gold or yellow paper using the letter patterns. Attach the caption to the top of the board as shown.

3. Print the Bible verse on white paper across the bottom of the board.

4. Enlarge the patterns, color them, and cut them out.

5. Mount the Baby Jesus pattern at the center of the board. Attach the animal patterns all around it.

6. You may want to attach hay or straw on the board to make the scene look more like a stable.

Suggested Activities

- Let younger students pretend to be the animals at the manger scene. Encourage them to show what they think the animals felt that night. Did they know what was happening?

- Sing the Christmas carol "Away in a Manger," but use the words "The Way in a Manger."

- Ask a volunteer to explain what a manger is. *(a food trough for animals)* Then ask students to explain why they think Mary and Joseph chose such a strange item to be Jesus' first bed. Ask them to think of other ways Mary and Joseph had to "adapt" and make the best of things that night. *(no beds, animals in the room, bad smells, dirt, etc.)*

- Let students choose partners. Give each pair a copy of the Bible verse, John 14:6, printed on a strip of paper and cut into 10 pieces. Have them compete to see who can put the words in correct order most quickly.

Patterns

Patterns

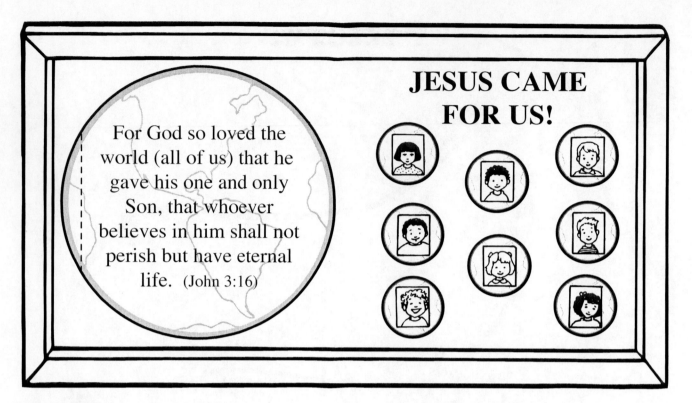

For God so loved the world (all of us) that he gave his one and only Son, that whoever believes in him shall not perish but have eternal life. (John 3:16)

JESUS CAME FOR US!

Materials

- green background paper
- white and red paper
- letter patterns on pages 143 and 144 *(optional)*
- patterns on pages 111 and 112
- scissors
- tape or stapler
- colored markers
- glue
- student photos

Directions

1. Cover the board with green paper.

2. Print out the caption or cut letters from red paper using the letter patterns. Attach the caption to the top of the board as shown.

3. Enlarge the patterns, color them, and cut them out.

4. Attach the baby Jesus pattern to the board.

5. Attach the world on top of the Jesus pattern at the left side only so it can be flipped open.

6. Copy the small world patterns, one for each student. Have them color and cut them out, then each glue his or her photo or self portrait on the world.

7. Have them add their worlds to the right side of the board.

Suggested Activities

- Read the Bible verse together, having each student say his or her name in the verse to personalize it. (Example: For God so loved <u>Karinne</u> that he gave his one and only Son, that if <u>Karinne</u> believes in him, <u>Karinne</u> shall not perish but have eternal life.)

- Give each older student two sheets of paper. Have them fold the paper in half, then staple them together along the left side to make a booklet. Challenge them to print a few words or phrase of John 3:16 on the bottom of each page of the booklet. On the rest of the page they can draw a picture to illustrate it to make the meaning of the verse clear. They can come up with a title for the booklet and print it on the front cover. Encourage them to give their booklets to friends or relatives who don't know Jesus.

- Pray together, encouraging children to express their thanks to God for sending Jesus for them.

Pattern

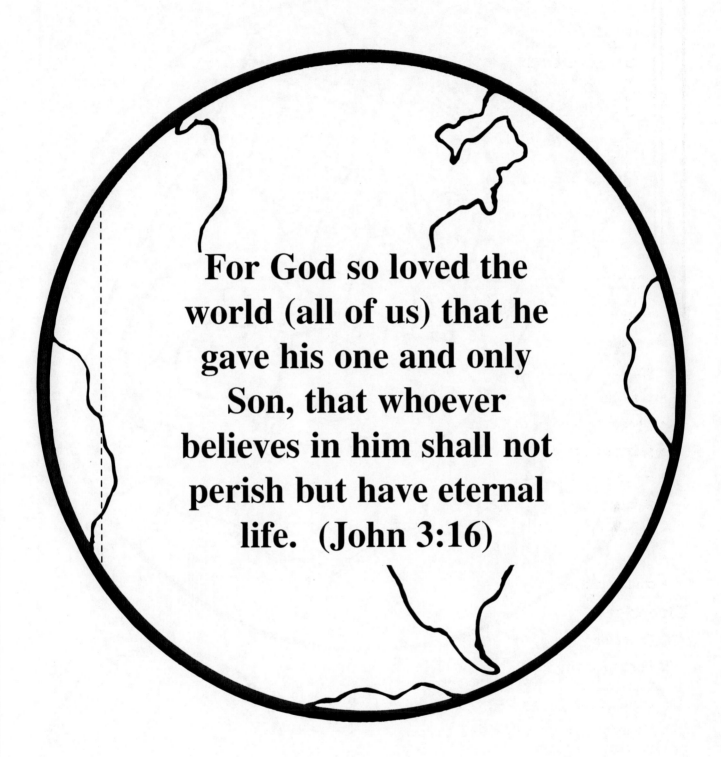

For God so loved the world (all of us) that he gave his one and only Son, that whoever believes in him shall not perish but have eternal life. (John 3:16)

Patterns

Jesus was born Lord of all

from the highest heaven

to the deepest sea!

Praise the Lord from the heavens . . . Praise the Lord . . . you great sea creatures and all ocean depths. (see Psalm 148:1,7)

Materials

- dark blue background paper
- white paper
- letter patterns on pages 143 and 144 *(optional)*
- patterns on pages 114–116
- scissors
- tape or stapler
- colored markers
- star stickers
- glue
- fish-shaped crackers *(optional)*

Directions

1. Cover the board with dark blue paper.

2. Print out the caption on white paper or cut letters from white paper using the letter patterns. Attach the caption to the top and bottom of the board as shown.

3. Enlarge the Bible verse pattern, cut it out, and attach it to the bottom of the board.

4. Enlarge the solar system and ocean animal patterns, color them, and cut them out.

5. Attach the solar system patterns to the top left of the board and the ocean animal patterns to the bottom right as shown. Draw wavy lines on the ocean portion to look like water.

6. Let some children stick small stars to the "highest heaven" portion of the board while others glue fish-shaped crackers or hand-drawn fish to the "deepest sea" portion.

Suggested Activities

- Ask students to share their ideas about what it means that Jesus came to be "Lord of all." Older students can look up and read John 1:1–3 and talk about Jesus, the Creator.

- Cut two large Christmas tree shapes from green paper. Mount each on a wall. Let children draw and cut out space items (stars, planets) to decorate one tree and ocean items (sea creatures) to decorate the other tree.

- Challenge older students to work in small groups to create raps or action rhymes praising Jesus for being Lord of all. They can perform their work for one another.

Patterns

114

Patterns

Patterns

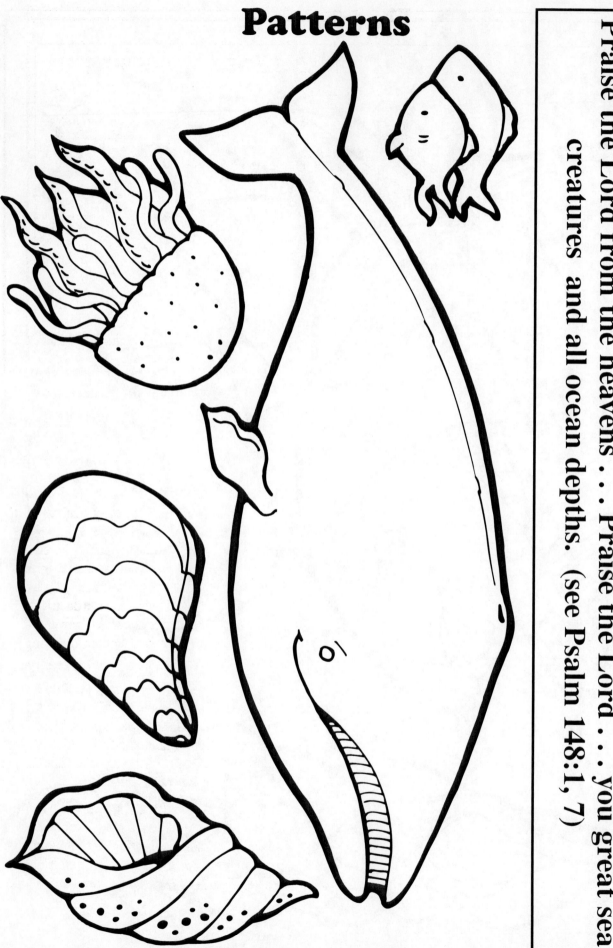

Praise the Lord from the heavens . . . Praise the Lord . . . you great sea creatures and all ocean depths. (see Psalm 148:1, 7)

God showers His children with blessings!

I will send down showers in season;
there will be showers of blessing. (Ezekiel 34:26b)

Materials

- bright blue background paper
- white and yellow paper
- light blue paper *(optional)*
- letter patterns on pages 143 and 144 *(optional)*
- patterns on pages 118 and 119
- scissors
- tape or stapler
- colored markers

Directions

1. Cover the board with bright blue paper.

2. Print out the caption or cut letters from yellow paper using the letter patterns. Attach the caption to the top of the board as shown.

3. Print the Bible verse across the bottom of the board.

4. Enlarge the picture of the two girls under the umbrella. Color it and cut it out. Attach it to the center of the board.

5. Make several copies of the small umbrellas and raindrops on white or light blue paper.

6. Give each student an umbrella on which to write a blessing he or she has received from God. They can scatter the umbrellas all over the board.

7. Let students cut out raindrops and add them to the board.

Suggested Activities

- Explain that a shower is not just rain, but it means a large amount of something. When a woman has a baby, her friends give her a shower, a party where many gifts are given to her for her newborn. God has showered us with many blessings. Let students tell about some blessings God has showered upon them. Then pray together, thanking God for His blessings.

- Have older students compete in a Bible drill, trying to find the following verses about blessings as quickly as possible: Psalm 29:11; Romans 10:12; Ezekiel 34:26; Matthew 5:9; Proverbs 28:20; Genesis 22:18; Isaiah 30:18; Revelation 1:3

- Have students think of ways they can share God's blessings with others. (Examples: share clothes or toys with children who have less, share salvation by telling friends about Jesus) Encourage them to share them soon.

Pattern

Patterns

In SPRINGTIME
We See God's Goodness Everywhere!

He has made everything beautiful in its time. (Ecclesiastes 3:11a)

Materials

- blue and green background paper
- white, yellow, and green paper
- letter patterns on pages 143 and 144 (optional)
- patterns on page 121
- scissors
- tape or stapler
- colored markers

Directions

1. Cover the top of the board with blue paper the middle with green paper, and the bottom with blue paper.

2. Print the caption or cut letters from yellow paper using the letter patterns. Attach the caption to the top of the board.

3. Print the Bible verse across the bottom of the board.

4. Use markers to draw a springtime scene on the board, or cut out simple shapes for a sun, tree, fish, etc. and arrange them on the board as shown. Draw wavy lines on the blue paper at the bottom of the board to make it look like water.

5. Enlarge the duck pattern for the mother duck; reduce it and make three or four copies for the baby ducks. Color them, cut them out, and attach them to the water on the board.

6. Make copies of the flower patterns for students to color, cut out, and add to the scene on the board. They can cut stems and leaves from green paper.

Suggested Activities

- If possible, take children outside for a short walk. Encourage them to notice signs of spring and be thankful for them. When you get back inside, pray together, thanking God for springtime.

- Make two copies of a flower pattern for each student. Help them staple the flowers together on the left side, then create a card to encourage someone who is sick or alone. Older students can use Bible concordances to find Bibles verses to write on their cards.

- Ask older students to write about how God makes us "beautiful" (holy) when we believe in Jesus. They will need to consider what a truly "beautiful" Christian is.

Patterns

Materials

- blue and green background paper
- white and red paper
- letter patterns on pages 143 and 144 *(optional)*
- pattern on page 123
- scissors
- tape or stapler
- colored markers
- cotton balls
- glue
- string and bits of fabric

Directions

1. Cover the board with blue paper. Overlap some green paper at the bottom.

2. Print the caption on white paper or cut letters from red paper using the letter patterns. Attach the caption to the top of the board.

3. Print the saying across the bottom of the board.

4. Enlarge the boy pattern, color it, and cut it out.

5. Attach the boy pattern to the board as shown.

6. Ask some students to cut large kite shapes from paper and color them in a variety of colors.

7. Mount the kites on the board.

8. Attach string from the kites to the boy's hands. Then attach short lengths of string with bits of fabric for kite tails.

9. Pull apart cotton balls and glue them to the board for clouds.

Suggested Activities

- Discuss the saying at the bottom of the board. Explain that doubt makes us hold back from doing what the Lord wants, but faith helps us trust Him to work through us.

- Give each child a small kite shape to decorate. Provide string and fabric bits for a tail. Have them print the sentence at the bottom of the board on their kites and use them for bookmarks.

- Ask older students to suggest some things God wants them to do that requires faith. *(Examples: tell others about Jesus, forgive those who have wronged them, believe His promises, etc.)*

Pattern

Summertime is growing time!

Thank you, God, for rain and sun that makes food grow for everyone.

Materials

- green background paper
- white and dark blue paper
- letter patterns on pages 143 and 144 *(optional)*
- pattern on page 125
- scissors
- tape or stapler
- colored markers
- gardening catalogs to be cut apart

Directions

1. Cover the board with green paper.

2. Print the caption on white paper or cut letters from dark blue paper using the letter patterns. Attach the caption to the top of the board.

3. Print the rhyme across the bottom of the board.

4. Enlarge the rabbit pattern, color it, cut it out, and attach it to the board as shown.

5. Let children cut pictures of vegetables and flowers of all kinds from gardening catalogs and add them to the board as part of the rabbit's garden.

Suggested Activities

- Let children tell about the flower or vegetable gardens at their homes. Children who live on farms can tell what grows there. Then read Matthew 6:28–33 aloud and discuss it. Ask children who makes things grow. Who takes care of us as well as all growing things? We can trust God to care for us in every way.

- Challenge older students to suggest ways they can "grow" this summer that would please the Lord. (Obviously, this includes more than physical growth, but can mean growth in obeying, reading the Bible, praying, witnessing, displaying godly character, etc.)

- Let younger children pretend they are plants (of their choice) growing from tiny sprouts (squatting down) to tall, healthy plants (standing tall with hands over heads). Let them do this to music.

- Have students write how they think Adam and Eve felt when they saw plants growing and discovered they could pick them and eat them. What plants did they eat? How did they like the taste? Did they thank God?

Pattern

Materials

- light green background paper
- white, yellow, green, and tan paper
- letter patterns on pages 143 and 144 *(optional)*
- patterns on page 127
- scissors
- tape or stapler
- colored markers (including black and brown)

Directions

1. Cover the board with light green paper.

2. Print the caption or cut letters from yellow paper using the letter patterns. Outline them with black or brown marker, then attach the caption to the top of the board.

3. Print the Bible verse across the bottom of the board.

4. Make flowers by cutting out three large circles and petals to go around them as shown. Attach them to the board with stems and leaves made from green paper.

5. Enlarge the three patterns to fit on the flower circles, color them, cut them out, and attach them to the flowers as shown.

6. Cut three circles from tan paper to fit over the center of the flowers. Number the circles 1, 2, and 3. Attach them over the flower centers on the left side only so they can be flipped open to see the pictures underneath.

Suggested Activities

- Talk about the pictures inside the flowers. Ask students to explain what they think the children are doing and how this can help them get to know Jesus better. Have them suggest other ways they can get to know Jesus better.

- Have children sing the second stanza of "I Will Make You Fishers of Men." (Read your Bible, pray every day, pray every day, pray every day. Read your Bible, pray every day, and you'll grow, grow, grow.)

- Have students design posters illustrating the importance of reading the Bible, praying, and going to church. Display the posters in a hallway for everyone to see.

- Pray together, encouraging students to commit themselves to getting to know Jesus better.

Patterns

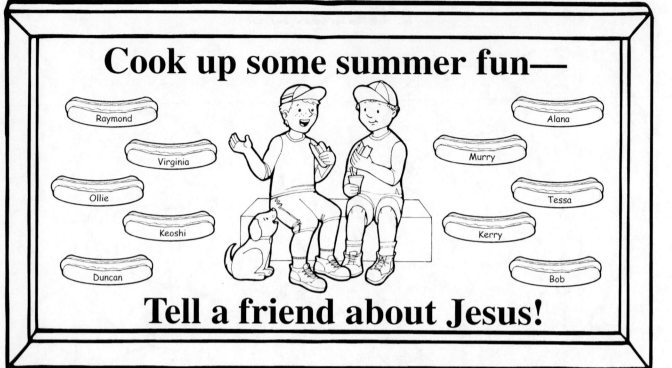

Cook up some summer fun—
Tell a friend about Jesus!

(Hot dog labels: Raymond, Virginia, Ollie, Keoshi, Duncan, Alana, Murry, Tessa, Kerry, Bob)

Materials

- yellow background paper
- white and red paper
- letter patterns on pages 143 and 144 (optional)
- patterns on page 129
- tape or stapler
- scissors
- colored markers

Directions

1. Cover the board with yellow paper.

2. Print the caption on white paper or cut letters from red paper using the letter patterns. Attach the caption to the top and bottom of the board.

3. Enlarge the pattern of the two boys, color it, cut it out, and attach it to the center.

4. Enlarge the hot dog pattern and give a copy to each student. Have each student color it and write on it the name of an unsaved friend to tell about Jesus.

5. Scatter the hot dogs all over the board.

Suggested Activities

- Ask students what fun things they do with friends during the summer (cookouts, swimming, playing ball, biking, etc.). Point out that every time they are with friends having fun, they can tell them about Jesus or invite them to church to hear about Jesus. That does not mean they need to be preachy, but just willing to share that Jesus loves them.

- Divide students into pairs. Challenge each pair to come up with a skit to show how they could tell a friend about Jesus or invite him or her to church. One of the students can be the friend and the other can be the one to tell or invite. Have each pair perform their skit for the rest of the group.

- Let volunteers share who first told them about Jesus or invited them to church.

- Let students help plan a special group get-together they can invite unsaved friends to. Let them suggest activities and games to play as well as food they can bring to share. Plan a simple program: students saying Bible verses, telling what they have learned about Jesus, and singing. You may want to schedule it during your regular meeting time to avoid schedule conflicts.

Patterns

The Autumn Season Is Full of Reasons to Honor God

Honor the Lord with . . . the firstfruits of all your crops.
(Proverbs 3:9)

Materials

- light green background paper
- orange and white paper
- black marker
- patterns on pages 131 and 132
- letter patterns on pages 143 and 144 (optional)
- crayons or colored markers
- scissors
- large envelope
- tape or stapler

Directions

1. Cover the board with light green paper.

2. Print out the caption or cut letters from orange paper using the letter patterns. Attach the caption to the top of the board.

3. Print the Bible verse on an orange paper strip and attach it to the bottom of the board.

4. Enlarge the patterns, color them, and cut them out.

5. Attach the farmer to the board as shown. Scatter pumpkins and corn stalks around the board.

6. Place additional pumpkin copies in an envelope taped or stapled underneath the board. When students think of reasons to honor the Lord in the autumn, they can print them on the pumpkins and place them in the farmer's wheelbarrow. As more are added, they will need to be stacked up.

Suggested Activities

- Play a game of "pumpkin blessings." Seat students in a circle. Give one a paper pumpkin. Play some praise music. The student passes the pumpkin to the next person in the circle, who passes it on, and so on. When the music stops, whoever has the pumpkin must honor God by telling one way He has recently blessed his or her family.

- Autumn is a beautiful time of year when we notice the natural world more. Take students outside to collect autumn leaves. Decorate the room with them and praise God.

Patterns

Patterns

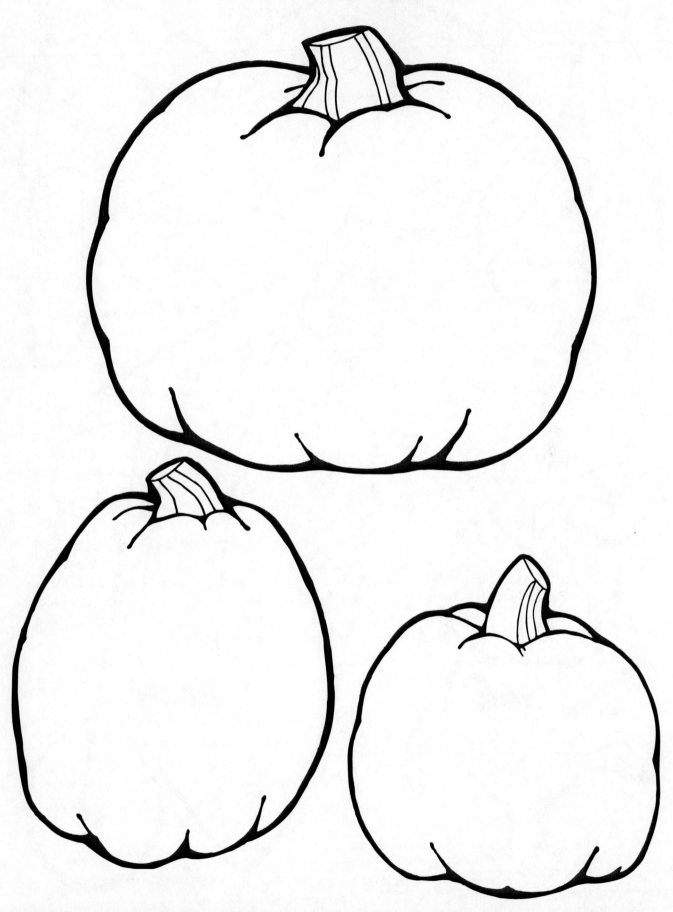

AUTUMN IS AMAZING!

THANK YOU GOD

God richly provides us with everything for our enjoyment. (see 1 Timothy 6:17b)

Materials

- light blue background paper
- white, red, orange, yellow, and light brown paper
- patterns on pages 134 and 135
- letter patterns on pages 143 and 144 *(optional)*
- crayons or colored markers
- scissors
- tape or stapler
- real autumn leaves *(optional)*

Directions

1. Cover the board with light blue paper.

2. Print out the caption on yellow paper or cut letters from fall colors using the letter patterns. Attach the caption to the top of the board.

3. Make enough copies of the acorn patterns on light brown paper for each letter of the bottom line of the caption. Enlarge them as necessary. Print a letter on each acorn and attach them to the board as shown.

4. Print the Bible verse at the bottom of the board.

5. Enlarge the picture pattern, color it, and cut it out. Attach it to the center of the board.

6. Enlarge the leaf patterns and give one to each child to trace and cut from colored paper. Scatter them all over the board.

7. Make additional copies of leaves on fall colors, or have children gather real leaves of various colors, for a border.

Suggested Activities

- Let children tell about their favorite "fall" things (cooler weather, colored leaves, harvest, weiner roasts, pumpkins, etc.). Read the Bible verse at the bottom of the board together, then pray, thanking God for this amazing time of year.

- Print the word "AUTUMN" vertically on the board. Challenge students to create an acrostic by coming up with words to describe the season. Each word must begin with a letter of the word on the board.

- Have older students work in pairs to create, then perform, raps or action rhymes about the glories of autumn God gives us to enjoy.

Pattern

Patterns

Winter–Spring–Summer–and Fall,

Always try to be kind to each other. (1 Thessalonians 5:15b)

God wants us to be kind to all.

Materials

- silver background paper
- white and light purple paper
- patterns on pages 137 and 138
- letter patterns on pages 143 and 144 (*optional*)
- crayons or colored markers
- tape or stapler
- scissors

Directions

1. Cover the board with silver paper to represent ice.

2. Print out the caption or cut letters from light purple paper using the letter patterns. Attach the caption to the top and bottom of the board.

3. Enlarge the patterns, color them, and cut them out. Make two or three copies of the single skater depending on the size of your board. Color them differently.

4. Attach the Bible verse sign at the left side of the board.

5. Put the penguin helping another at the center of the board. Position the other skaters around the board as space allows.

Suggested Activities

- Let children study the bulletin board and make up a story about it. Why did the skater fall? Why is only one penguin helping that one up? Help them relate the imaginary situation to real-life everyday situations in which they can show kindness to others.

- Ask older students to brainstorm specific situations that may occur in winter in which God can use them to show kindness to others. (Examples: A schoolmate may not have a good winter coat, an older neighbor may not be strong enough to clear ice or snow off the sidewalk.) Encourage students to look for kindness opportunities and do what God wants them to do to make this season a little easier or more pleasant for other people. (If time permits, students can brainstorm situations for the other seasons too.)

- Sing this song to the tune of "If You're Happy and You Know It."

  Be kind to each other all the time.
  Be kind to each other all the time.
  Don't you know that God wants you to be kind in all you do?
  So be kind to each other all the time.

Pattern

Patterns

Always try to be kind to each other.

(1 Thessalonians 5:15b)

138

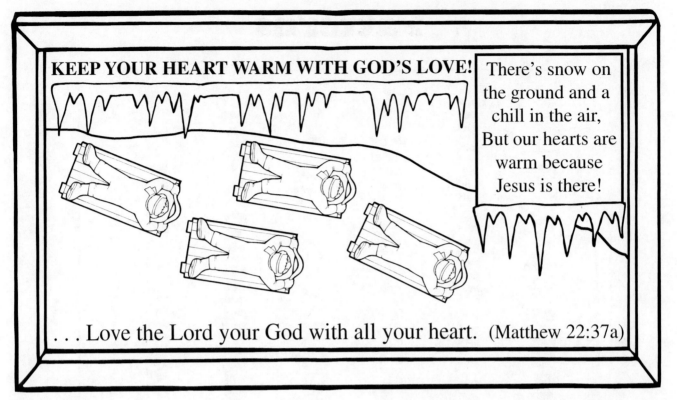

KEEP YOUR HEART WARM WITH GOD'S LOVE!

There's snow on the ground and a chill in the air, But our hearts are warm because Jesus is there!

. . . Love the Lord your God with all your heart. (Matthew 22:37a)

Materials

- white and blue background paper
- white paper
- patterns on page 140
- letter patterns on pages 143 and 144 *(optional)*
- tape or stapler
- crayons or colored markers
- scissors

Directions

1. Cover the board by making a snow-covered hill of white paper and a sky of blue.

2. Print the caption on white paper or cut out letters using the letter patterns, outlining each letter with black marker. Attach the caption to the top of the board.

3. Print the Bible verse at the bottom of the board.

4. Make several copies of the child on the sled pattern. Color them different colors, cut them out, and attach them to the board at various places on the white hill.

5. Enlarge the poem box and attach it to the right side of the board as shown.

6. Just for fun, draw icicle shapes hanging from the bottom of some of the caption letters and the poem box.

Suggested Activities

- Let children share their winter fun experiences, such as sledding, ice skating, etc. Talk about how cold we can get when we stay outside a long time. Explain that our bodies may get cold, but when we know Jesus as Savior, our hearts never get cold. Jesus warms out hearts with His love. He wants us to love Him with all our heart.

- Challenge older students to consider how being a Christian is like riding a sled down a snow covered hill. See what analogies they can come up with. (Example: Christians trust God to take them through life similar to the way a sledder trusts the sled to take him down the slope.)

- Print this statement on the board: "God takes a person's cold heart, frozen by sin, and melts it with His love." Have students draw cartoon strips to illustrate that concept.

Patterns

There's snow on
the ground and a
chill in the air,
But our hearts
are warm because
Jesus is there!

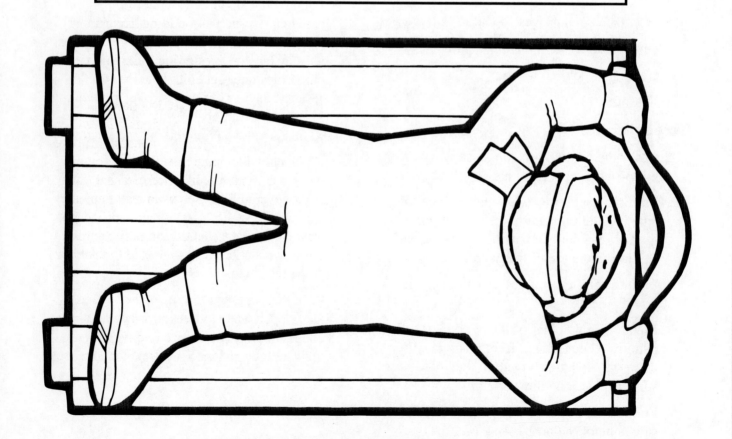

Look at the snow and remember God's forgiveness!

Wash me and I will be whiter than snow. (Psalm 51:7b)

Materials

- dark blue background paper
- white paper
- patterns on page 142
- letter patterns on pages 143 and 144 *(optional)*
- crayons or colored markers
- scissors
- tape or stapler
- fabric and buttons
- glue
- cotton balls

Directions

1. Cover the board with dark blue paper.

2. Print the caption or cut letters from white paper using the letter patterns. Attach the caption to the top of the board.

3. Print the Bible verse at the bottom of the board.

4. Enlarge the snowman and snow child patterns, color them, cut them out, and attach them to the board.

5. To add dimension to the board, glue fabric to the snow people's hats and scarves. Glue buttons on them for facial features.

6. Let students tear white paper or cotton balls into small pieces and attach them to the board for snowflakes.

Suggested Activities

- Provide students with paper, markers, scissors, and glue, and let them create their own personal copies of the bulletin board display to take home.

- God promises in His Word to not only forgive our sins, but to wash us whiter than snow. If possible, bring a container of pure white snow for students to see so they can catch a glimpse of how God cleanses us from our sin and wants us to stay pure and clean. The Bible describes sin as dirty and ugly while righteousness (right living) is clean and pure. Have students suggest ways to stay pure like snow (pray, read the Bible, obey God, etc.).

- Have older students look up these verses about God's forgiveness and cleansing in their Bibles and read them aloud: Isaiah 1:18; Hebrews 1:3; 1 John 1:7, 9. Let them thank God for His forgiveness.

Patterns

Letter Patterns

Letter Patterns

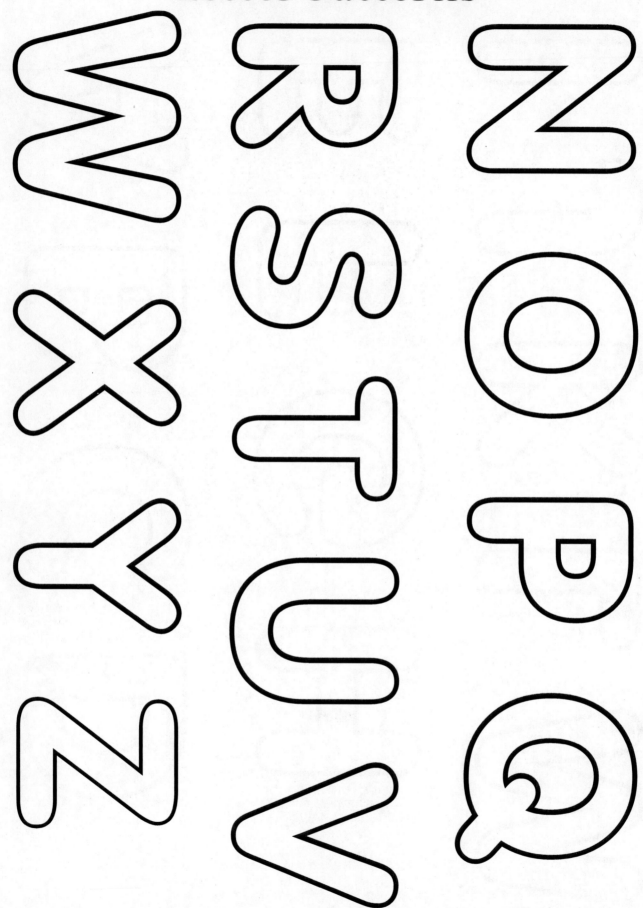